NO SECOND CHANCES

NO SECOND CHANCES

THE INSIDE STORY OF THE CAMPAIGN FOR A SECOND EU REFERENDUM

MORGAN JONES

Biteback Publishing

First published in Great Britain in 2026 by
Biteback Publishing Ltd, London

ISBN 978-1-78590-983-2

10 9 8 7 6 5 4 3 2 1

A CIP catalogue record for this book is available from the British Library.

Set in Minion Pro and Elizeth

Printed and bound in Great Britain by
CPI Group (UK) Ltd, Croydon CR0 4YY

FSC
www.fsc.org
MIX
Paper | Supporting responsible forestry
FSC® C013604

CONTENTS

CAST OF CHARACTERS

Charlie Atkins, People's Vote staffer

Tom Baldwin, director of communications at the People's Vote campaign

Steve Bray, aka 'Stop Brexit Man', SODEM founder

Richard Brooks, co-founder of For our Future's Sake

Louise Brown, co-founder of North East for Europe

Tom Brufatto, chair of Britain for Europe

Mike Buckley, founder of Labour for a People's Vote

Ben Chambers, founder and host of the *Single Minded Rejoiners* radio show and podcast (formerly *Sixteen Million Rising*)

Michael Chessum, national spokesperson for Another Europe is Possible

Amanda Chetwynd-Cowieson, co-founder of For our Future's Sake

Luke Cooper, co-founder of Another Europe is Possible

Hugo Dixon, founder of InFacts

Brendan Donnelly, leader of the Rejoin EU Party

Will Dry, co-founder of Our Future Our Choice

Drew Galdron, Boris Johnson impersonator

Mike Galsworthy, co-founder of Scientists for EU

Mike Gapes, Labour MP until February 2019, then Change UK MP

Colin Gordon, Oxford for Europe activist

Patrick Heneghan, CEO of the European Movement (early 2019) and interim CEO of Open Britain (late 2019)

Flo Hutchings, Best for Britain staffer

Patrick Jenkins, Labour for a People's Vote staffer

Sarah Jones, online anti-Brexit personality known as 'Sarah Saboteur'

Madeleina Kay, 'EU Supergirl' activist

Gareth Kearns, SODEM activist

Matt Kelly, creator and editor-in-chief of the *New European*

Mark Kieran, interim CEO of the Renew Party (2018–19) and CEO of Open Britain (2020–present)

Bashir Ibrahim, People's Vote staffer

Andrew Lewin, founder of Remain Labour

Dorian Lynskey, co-host of the *Remainiacs* podcast

James McGrory, director of the People's Vote campaign

Felix Marquardt, who facilitated the foundation of Our Future Our Choice

Jolyon Maugham, founder of the Good Law Project and Spring the Party

Anand Menon, director of UK in a Changing Europe

Annabel Mullin, founder and leader of the Advance Together Party (2017–20), leader of the Renew Party (2018–19) and Change UK European election candidate (2019)

Luke Myer, For our Future's Sake staffer

Femi Oluwole, co-founder of Our Future Our Choice

Laura Parker, private secretary to Jeremy Corbyn (2016–17) and national coordinator for Momentum (2017–19)

Roland Rudd, chair of Open Britain

James Schneider, director of strategic communications to Jeremy Corbyn (2016–19)

Ed Shackle, Our Future Our Choice staffer

Naomi Smith, co-host of *Remainiacs* and CEO of Best for Britain (2019–present)

Antony So, People's Vote staffer

Lara Spirit, co-founder of Our Future Our Choice

Ros Taylor, co-host of *Remainiacs*

Eloise Todd, co-founder and CEO (2017–19) of Best for Britain

Maggie Turner, Bath for Europe activist and inventor of the bEUret

Yvonne Wancke, co-founder of North East for Europe

Richard Wilson, Leeds for Europe activist

Sue Wilson, chair of Bremain in Spain

Amelia Womack, deputy leader of the Green Party (2014–22) and co-founder of Another Europe is Possible

INTRODUCTION

Maggie Turner invented something you will be familiar with, even if you don't know its name. The item she created became ubiquitous in the anti-Brexit world, a cultural symbol so potent and recognisable, so – in the true sense of the word – iconic, that it is now in the collection of the British Museum.

Turner, who had moved to Bath with her husband when he retired, having spent much of her life in London, had been 'devastated' by the result of the Brexit vote in June 2016. By the autumn of 2016 she had become heavily involved with a local group called Bath for Europe. 'There were a lot of talented people, tech-savvy people and people good at marketing [and] publicity,' in the group, which Turner describes as very active, with a core of around a dozen people organising speakers and street stalls and generally agitating against Brexit. They weren't acting in isolation: around the country, people who'd never before been particularly political were taking to the streets over Brexit, talking and thinking about politics in a way they hadn't before. Fairly quickly, by October or November of 2016, the group 'got merchandise', Turner remembers. 'And then I thought, well, I wonder what I could do… would a hat be a good idea?'

She thought about it further and eventually, inspiration struck: 'Perhaps I saw a beret or something on somebody and I thought, "God, that could actually work," and so I made this, my first prototype.' Speaking on Zoom, she held the prototype up to the camera. I was looking at a blue beret with yellow stars stuck around the edge. This was one of the last of the almost seventy interviews I conducted for this book; by the time I spoke to Turner, I was very much immersed in the world of the campaign for a second EU referendum. So much so, in fact, the transcript reveals that upon seeing the first prototype, I told her it was 'like looking at history'. Embarrassing, retrospectively, to catch oneself being starstruck by a hat, but I was.

In my defence, it was not just any hat. They were initially, Turner explains, called the 'Original Bath Beret', owing to their city of origin, but shortly afterwards were redubbed the 'bEUret' (you just say it like beret). At first, Turner bought berets from Amazon and a team of volunteers sat around her kitchen table sticking the stars on by hand. 'They were immediately so popular,' she explains. 'I remember we went on our first march and we sold sixty.'

They had a hit on their hands and couldn't keep on producing them in Turner's house. They needed to scale up. As Turner remembers, 'We realised that we were going to have to formalise it, because we were selling quite a few, and I had to become a sole trader.' After that, she 'had to find somebody to manufacture them'. Turner says she 'tried all through Europe,' but it was 'really difficult. So I ended up in China.'

The process was 'really complicated, because when the first consignment of berets [came] over here, you [had] to pay import duty, transport costs, VAT, custom charges.' But once the mass-produced bEUrets had arrived, they were in business. People began to order them online. Turner says, 'We were sending them to Europe. I've sent them to America, and we were sending them all over the country.' She thinks a grand total of 4,807 berets were sold that way, through online shipment; if you ordered one, you would also get some anti-Brexit currency that they'd mocked up. Turner showed me these, too. One featured Boris Johnson. 'That's the Bank of Brexit Lies, three hundred and fifty million,' Turner explains, a reference to the infamous 'We send the EU £350 million a week, let's fund our NHS instead' campaign bus. Another, from the 'Imperial Bank of Brexit', featured former Tory MP Jacob Rees-Mogg.

As well as selling the bEUrets online, at other times Turner and her fellow activists would simply bring large quantities of them to anti-Brexit demonstrations to sell there. For the big London marches, Turner would 'park the car on Park Lane and [it] would be absolutely bunged full of these berets in Lidl carrier bags'.

The berets were sold for a tenner. The money covered the production costs, with the rest going to a range of anti-Brexit organisations. Turner says they gave a total of £38,000 to organisations including Open Britain, Our Future Our Choice (OFOC), For our Future's Sake (FFS), SODEM, Led by Donkeys, the Good Law Project, Britain for Europe and the People's Vote itself. Of these, Turner and the bEUret team had a particularly close relationship with SODEM, Steve Bray's protest group, who they would often join on Parliament Square. 'We got to know them. We gave them loads of berets to sell,' Turner remembers.

In addition to selling them, supporters would often try to get them into the hands (and onto the heads) of movement notables. As Turner remembers, 'People gave them to Ian Dunt, Dominic Grieve, Alastair Campbell, James O'Brien. I wrote to the Ukrainian embassy and asked that they send it on to [Volodymyr] Zelensky.' While a picture exists of Campbell donning one of the blue hats, I have yet to see evidence that Zelensky has made use of this gift. The bEUret joined Instagram in January 2019; posts show bales of new stock, alongside activists and celebrities – both micro and otherwise, from Bob Geldof to Femi Oluwole – posing with the hats.

The Brexit years were hectic for Turner and her comrades. 'We were just so busy,' she explains. 'We went on all the major marches in London: there was the Unite [for Europe] march in 2017, the People's Vote march in June '18, the People's Vote march in October '18, the Rejoin March, we went to Lib Dem conferences, went to Conservative conferences, went to the Cheltenham rallies.' As Bath for Europe's members were, unsurprisingly, based in Bath, a frequent target for their protests was Jacob Rees-Mogg, then the MP for North West Somerset, who lived 'about ten miles away'. Turner remembers 'going around his area and getting moved away by the police'.

One particular high point took place at the Last Night of the Proms in 2018, when Turner and the bEUret team conspired with a group called the EU Flag Mafia (most famous as the source of the rectangular yellow 'Bollocks to Brexit' stickers). The Flag Mafia had given out flags, and Turner supplied them with 'over 500 berets' to give to attendees of the Proms. 'There were so many of these berets, all these people wearing the berets. And you know, it was really good, because it was quite international, and the BBC couldn't do anything about it and everyone got really upset.' Turner's attitude here chimed with those of many I spoke to: the strange, anarchic and stubborn spirit of older, previously not hugely political, people doing activism, often viewing getting under the right people's skin as a victory in and of itself.

In the years after the Brexit vote, the bEUret became shorthand for a whole cultural and political movement: the battle armour of the ardent Remainer who refuses to give up the cause. Directly after the vote in June 2016, the likes of Turner were essentially out on their own, with a Conservative majority in Parliament making it look like Theresa May would have a comparatively straightforward time of it passing a Brexit deal. After Labour's surprisingly strong performance at the 2017 election, however – depriving May of her majority, off the back, in good part, of voters unhappy about Brexit, despite Labour having no pledge to reverse it – a political space opened up to contest Brexit.

Parliament simultaneously ground to a halt and went into overdrive over how, exactly, we would be leaving the European

Union; while there was as much attention on Westminster as there's ever been, it was getting next to nothing done. I spoke to a think-tank researcher who was at the time working to 'track all the different bills that were going through Parliament'. It was, they noted, 'really striking' how much 'everything other than Brexit had ground to a halt'. At one point in 2019, they say, 'If I recall correctly, the only government bill going through Parliament was the Animals in Circuses Bill, which my manager took great glee in telling me applied to, I think, a total of eleven animals, including a snake called Steve.' As the journalist Henry Mance put it, 'Between the general elections of 2017 and 2019, Britain was suspended in mid-air.'[1] In this vacuum, Turner and co. became the foot soldiers of the anti-Brexit push.

The tool that this push ultimately swung behind was a new vote, a second referendum on Brexit (although its advocates would generally discourage use of the term 'second referendum', viewing it as bad advertising for the proposal). The idea itself was coterminous with the initial decision to leave: once there was Brexit, there was a call for a new referendum. The barrister Jolyon Maugham would write about it on his blog on 24 June 2016, and a petition calling for a new vote was quickly launched: 'We the undersigned call upon HM Government to implement a rule that if the Remain or Leave vote is less than 60 per cent based on a turnout less than 75 per cent there should be another referendum.' This was somewhat different in form to later campaigns, which would focus on a vote on a final deal, but clearly springing from the same sentiments. The petition garnered 4,150,262 signatures and was debated on 5 September 2016.[2]

I lost count of the number of people I interviewed who used the bEUret as a synecdoche when talking about the protest base of the anti-Brexit movement. 'Lots of people at our marches weren't just Remainers but blue berets with yellow star Remainers,' explained one senior People's Vote staffer. Often, they spoke quite pejoratively as they did so. 'My strong view is that whatever we do to get back into the European Union' in future, one person I spoke to told me, 'it should not involve blue berets with yellow stars.' The emotions inspired by this fairly non-aesthetic hat get at the heart of the problems of the anti-Brexit movement, which, in the years after the referendum, coalesced around the demand for a new vote. It was a political movement whose (for want of a better word) elite had a tortured relationship with its base, simultaneously completely dependent on it and deeply embarrassed by it – not unlike today's Labour Party.

In his excellent 2019 *Guardian* article on the cultural world and excesses of diehard Remainers, the journalist Daniel Cohen coined the term 'Remainist'. Remainists are people who are not just exercised in their views on Europe but close to monomaniacal, dedicating themselves to a truly impressive degree to campaigning and protesting and talking about how much they wanted to stop Brexit. This monomania is often somewhat abstract from the European Union itself – indeed, I was struck in a handful of interviews with people who had spent years of their lives fighting Brexit by how shallow their thoughts on the institution itself were. As discussed further in Chapter 1, many felt it was a slight on their identity.

If you're trying to picture the Remainists in your mind's eye, you've probably imagined them wearing a bEUret. They were the base – the money, the meat in the room, the MP emailers – of a political movement that would eventually sway the Labour Party and the SNP to its view that Britain needed a new referendum on Europe and managed to swallow the Liberal Democrats whole (if you remember, the party fought the 2019 election on a 'revoke' platform). Through fevered action and association, the 'Remainists' gave birth to the strange and distinctive culture that this book explores. I would contend that this culture took on more import than might have been expected for two reasons: firstly, because Brexit was so often understood in cultural as well as purely political terms, and, more mundanely, because despite gripping the nation, the political side of Brexit was not exciting to look at and so the more colourful manifestations of anti-Brexit sentiment received outsized coverage in the press.

Many books about politics purport to be able to put the reader 'in the room where it happens'. Various journalists are better- or worse-sourced, of course, and some can get closer to decisions than others, but I've never really liked this way of seeing politics, as contained in some far-off room to which you need to pick a sherpa-like guide and hope they can get you there. It's undeniable that political decisions are made in rooms in Downing Street and Whitehall – or, for our purposes, around the copper-topped table at the Resolution

Foundation with Alastair Campbell and Peter Mandelson, or in Roland Rudd's offices on The Strand over what I'm told was 'fucking good coffee' – but political cultures are made in a far more diffuse and eclectic array of places. In Facebook groups; on the high streets of market towns; around Maggie Turner's kitchen table with the felt stars and cloth glue; on marches; at meetings; and at the performances of Dance Europa, Swindon for Europe's affiliated dance group, in Swindon town centre (there's a lot of swishing, if you were wondering).

The problem was, however, that the base and the culture they created was, well, kind of mad, out of touch with the country and made them often deeply alienating to advocates for their own cause. That this culture existed was notable and the times it existed in gave it exposure; that didn't necessarily make it politically useful. The politicians and operatives who wanted what the activists wanted – to stop Brexit – needed them, but they also kept them at arm's length, often treating them with something between embarrassment and disdain. In many ways, the ask that the anti-Brexit movement settled on and all ultimately swung behind – a new referendum – was a compromise between these two groups, pushing the grassroots activists to be more moderated (often somewhat unwillingly) and the political class to become more ambitious (somewhat ill-advisedly).

This problem of internal dissonance was summed up best by Tom Baldwin, the director of communications for the People's Vote campaign, who said that he felt the campaign he was so heavily involved in was 'at its best … a reaction to the mess that Brexit had become, and at its worst, an expression of a sort of Remain ideology'.[3]

I asked another People's Vote staffer how they would describe 'Remain ideology'. They detailed this worldview as such:

> Britain was quite a backwards country and as both a route to and a signalling of newfound openness, optimism and enlightenment, we joined the EU and did very, very well out of that, and it meant that we were closer together with all of our brilliant peers around Europe etc. and gave young people lots of opportunities, and unfortunately, a group of people who felt left behind by domestic, economic and political problems were fibbed to and used in order to ruin that for everyone else.

I think this is as good an elucidation as you will find of the worldview of the people who made up the mass of this mass movement. Perhaps crucial here is the belief that Brexit was based on lies, which is common to almost everyone in the space (there is a reason why Maggie Turner and co. decided to send people fake money from the 'Bank of Brexit lies'). The political scientist Rob Ford's run-down of the attitude focuses more neatly on the view anti-Brexit campaigners had of Leave voters: 'They were lied to, stupid. They are reactionary. They are wrong. The vote was not legitimate. The vote was not fair. They were misled by the media.'

Following on from the view that lies are central to understanding why Brexit happened are two things: the idea that it is therefore fundamentally illegitimate and that anyone who voted for it was in some way deceived, very possibly because they were underinformed or, as the subtext of many assertions that people are underinformed goes, simply dim. As the academics Jonathan Moss, Emily Robinson and Jake Watts describe in their Mass Observation study of how people felt about Brexit, *The Politics of Feeling in Brexit Britain*, 'In line with the dominant media narrative, Remain supporters frequently portrayed Leave voters as irrational, uneducated and motivated by negative emotions of fear and prejudice; they also expressed anger that they had made the "wrong" decision based on the "wrong" sources of information.'[4]

This perspective was not limited to the base of the movement and was widespread across many Remain-favouring groups, often even written into the accounts of the event. Academic and the author of a history of the 1975 referendum Robert Saunders has argued, 'Academics leaned heavily towards Remain in 2016,' and then and in the years since, 'much academic writing suggests a striking reluctance to engage with the opposing side as a serious moral or intellectual position.'[5] Having surveyed research on the subject, Anand Menon, director of the think tank UK in a Changing Europe, told me, 'What was absolutely staggering was the degree to which the academic literature's starting point was, "We're in the European Union. It's a good thing. Let's look at how it works."' To his view, 'We failed as a profession I think, pretty badly,' because there was such 'normative buy-in' to that premise, something which, he says, 'people are very reluctant to admit to'. The historian Richard Bourke rebuked these very attitudes – as somewhat exemplified, he argues, by the Irish writer Fintan O'Toole's 2018 book *Heroic Failure*, which discusses Brexit as the political fruit of post-war Britain's own misjudged self-conception as simultaneously underdog and top dog – when he argued, 'Secession from [the EU] might be a mistake, but it is hardly incomprehensible except by resort to a narrative of narrow-minded prejudice.'[6]

Resorting to this narrative is, if you're a historian or a political scientist, lazy. If you're a politician – or perhaps more correctly, someone attempting to do politics – it's absolutely fatal. 'Brexit made everyone feel like they were a political expert,' one People's Vote staffer told me, 'and not everyone is.' As the political scientist Rob Ford put it to me, 'I always think with any kind of political campaign, a good test is to imagine you were on the receiving end of it. What would your reaction be, right, if you were told you voted for this thing but actually you were duped? Would you be convinced by that?'

While many people working on the People's Vote campaign and in the wider movements were keenly aware of the problem of the patronising logic of a 'concentrate and ask again' approach to Brexit, implicit in campaigning for a new vote, it was never one they quite managed to solve. As one person involved in the campaign put it, despite 'superhuman' efforts from the comms team under Tom Baldwin, 'I don't think there is a way in which you say to however many million people you were wrong, without saying you were wrong.' There are, they say, 'better and worse ways of saying you were wrong, but fundamentally, you are just saying to someone you were wrong, and it's not that you were wrong ten years ago… you were wrong two years ago. And obviously you can say that without saying it's because you're a moron or it's because you're gullible or because you're thick, and it's better when you don't say any of those things. But you're still saying to somebody, you're wrong, right?' As Rob Ford puts it, 'Any campaign that was built around that impulse was doomed because you are starting from a position of not respecting the legitimacy of the choice that people who disagree with you made.'

These people at the top, in the anti-Brexit boardrooms, trying to square the circle of telling the nation they were wrong – who were they? The answer to this is the same as it would be in many political campaigns and parties, only perhaps more so: mostly white men of a certain age, who were, just like the people manning the street stalls, really feeling things about Britain leaving the European Union. In this category one finds Roland Rudd, the businessman who chaired the Open Britain board and his longstanding friend, the journalist Hugo Dixon; a bevy of New Labour grandees, including Alastair Campbell, Peter Mandelson and Andrew Adonis; former Labour spinner Tom Baldwin and former Lib Dem spinner James McGrory; Superdry owner Julian Dunkerton, who donated significant sums; and former Conservative health secretary Stephen Dorrell. They were people who had had successful careers and a nominally sound understanding of British politics. Their response to Brexit, however, was none too different from the denizens of Bath for Europe: they were horrified and they wanted to do something about it.

As one People's Vote staffer put it:

> I also think that for a lot of middle-aged, upper-middle-class men who had worked in politics but hadn't been successful politicians, it felt like this enormous opportunity, their '60s in Paris, like it was this moment where everything was up in the air and maybe, finally, everyone will listen to my really interesting ideas about proportional representation, you know. And that's quite a heady combination, I think, if you feel like people have stolen the thing that made you feel good about yourself but that that might present you with an opportunity to finally be fêted as the genius you are.

The people – mostly men – in this category would be central within the People's Vote campaign's rise to media and political prominence. They would also be the key players in the dramatic struggle for control which led to its implosion.

Perhaps all this is unsurprising. In one People's Vote staffer's reckoning, 'FOMO and vanity' motivated many of those involved at senior levels. 'I think FOMO and vanity and a sense of duty often are actually slightly more hand in hand than we like to think.' Another person involved in the campaign put a slightly harsher spin on it, noting that in recent years we've begun to have conversations about what to do with retired politicians, 'but we also just don't really know what to do with, like, retired heads of communications or retired special advisers.' Idle hands are the devil's playthings: Frank Sinatra can have a cold, but Alastair Campbell probably shouldn't have FOMO.

How well the whole thing went is a matter of debate: zero-sum outcomes (they did not secure a new vote and Britain left the European Union in January 2020) do somewhat obscure the successes of the campaign in shifting MPs and making the whole idea seem plausible. 'At the start, you could fit the MPs really up for it in the back of a cab,' Alastair Campbell has said.[7] That number grew significantly. In the House of Commons, amendments backing a new vote failed by small margins. The idea was taken seriously by the political mainstream. Henry Mance describes the People's Vote campaign as 'a case study in political near-misses'. Personally, while in some ways simply factual, this is not how I would assess the campaign, as I tend to think it over-weights the viability of a new vote.

Who am I? What are my motives in all of this? Why did I find myself moved to spend so much time considering the semiotics of the bEUret? Politically and professionally, I come from the Labour Party, a place famously obsessed with its own internal world. But say what you like about Labour's solipsism, the party has had time to work on it. Its psychodrama has been well over a century in the making. While drawing from many pre-existing strands and organisations, the campaign for a new referendum after the Brexit vote interests me because it was a political culture (and, in fact, many political organisations) built from scratch, one which rose and fell on fast forward in the glitchy years of the 2017–19 parliament. It had its own micro-celebrities, a distinctive visual culture (so distinctive that art historian Noni Stacey has written an entire book about the photography and art of the Brexit debate), its own slogans and hashtags and paraphernalia. In the reporting of this book, I saw an adult woman wearing a T-shirt that said '*Testiculae ad Brexitum*' on it. It means 'Bollocks to Brexit' in Latin. From a political communications standpoint, this is disastrous. From a cultural analysis angle, it's an incredibly rich text.

However, while I might find it a rich text – sufficiently rich to have interviewed dozens and dozens of people and spent countless hours writing and thinking about it – it is worth staking out here, in the Introduction, my view on it all, which is also, ultimately, the view of the book you are about to read. I came to the UK from Ireland in 2015. I voted to Remain and I hold only an Irish passport, but whatever my views on the referendum's outcome, I have never thought a second referendum was a good idea. I didn't think so at the time, when I was a student and then a junior political aide; I don't think so now, eight years and many interviews later. If you're of the second-vote persuasion, as many people reading this will no doubt be, you may disagree with me, perhaps violently, but tough. It's my book.

People will tell you they got close, they almost got it over the line, twelve votes in the House, more were in the pipeline, MPs were talking, they were softening, if only… I don't believe it. In as much as you can ever make definitive claims about the probability of events that did not happen, I do not believe the parliamentary maths was ever there. The People's Vote campaign was arguably (and impressively) more successful than it should have had any right to be, but there was a ceiling. All it was ever going to get was close. But just because something isn't possible, doesn't mean it isn't important. 'I often feel covering politics is a bit like covering the witch craze in early modern Germany,' says the journalist Stephen Bush. 'You've got to accept that people believe in witches, right? And they will make decisions that are not in their own interests [based on this belief].' To him, the campaign for a new vote was in this category, but that meant, viable or not, it was 'a serious force that I had to understand in order to understand and cover well both the passage of Brexit through the House of Commons and the fate of the Labour Party'.

That does not mean that I think the people involved in it were stupid or making a particularly drastic misjudgement. Many of them do not think it was a good idea themselves, whether they made that assessment at the time or with hindsight. 'In my heart of hearts I did not think a second referendum was a good idea,' says *Remainiacs* host Ros Taylor. Mike Buckley, who founded and ran the organisation Labour for a People's Vote, speculated that

> had Remain world remained more unified and focused… [but] we will never know the answers. My guess is [it would not have made a difference] because I suspect that enough MPs would have still thought, you know what, this is a bad

> idea. The people voted, that's democracy, right? And in the end, I've actually probably come around to those people's view.

Another person who spent years of their life working for a new referendum struck a similar note: 'The second referendum was the idealists' approach, and actually, the Lisa Nandys of this world, who know a thing or two about how to do politics, were probably right in pushing for a customs union, because that's where the arithmetic was politically.' Another who worked for various pro-second vote organisations said simply that they 'now don't actually believe we should have had a second referendum anyway,' adding that it likely 'would have made things worse'. But at the time, the witch craze was on. People were swept along by the momentum of the ask for a new vote.

Some people even suspect that the second referendum campaign was more than just a bad idea: it was an actively harmful one, which, by fostering a double-or-nothing mindset, stood in the way of a more moderated Brexit deal. Plenty of people, however, reject this framing, arguing that it presupposes a context that was in fact created by the People's Vote campaign and their allies. That is to say, a hypothetical softer Brexit is only politically imaginable to us because of the work put in and space created by anti-Brexit campaigners.

In Britain, Brexit was the defining event of the last decade, both politically but also, more so than almost any political event, culturally. People understood it at an identity level. By June 2018, Leave and Remain had already eclipsed party affiliations in a survey of political self-description: 'Voters are far more likely to declare a Brexit identity than they are to say that they have a party identity.'[8]

If you have lived in the UK in the intervening years, you will likely know what these identities mean and will have a ready cultural script of 'the unthinking Leave voter and the patronising Remainer'.[9] It's not always an especially accurate one – no script encompassing millions of people can be – but it is one that has informed our politics and our social understanding in the years hence. Much of the work to define this script, however, was done after the fact of the vote by, among others, the people featured in this book and by the culture the anti-Brexit movement created. This culture often left a more lasting impression than the politics it grew from – you can still recognise the bEUret, but you probably can't remember the details of the Kyle–Wilson amendment – and for people interested in class, activism, political communications and Brexit, it remains a rich text. *Testiculae ad Brexitum*, indeed.

PART I

THE CULTURE

CHAPTER 1

THE GRASSROOTS

The 2016 referendum result took many people by unpleasant surprise. In Newcastle, Yvonne Wancke was 'horrified, shocked' about what she described as 'probably one of the worst results that I've ever been aware of'. In Spain, where Sue Wilson has lived for eighteen years, she was 'completely shocked' and likened the process to grieving:

> I really can't say that I've been affected by something so strongly, other than a close death in the family before, so much so that it took me three weeks to regain my equilibrium. I was actually bursting into tears for no apparent reason, getting angry for no apparent reason.

In Leeds, Richard Wilson was 'appalled by the result of the referendum, absolutely appalled'. In Sunderland, Louise Brown had 'thought it would be fine' and woken up to a 'horrible result and a very unexpected result'. In Oxford, Colin Gordon hadn't been sure of a victory but had nonetheless found himself regarding the outcome with 'a level of shock'.

With the exception of Richard Wilson, a Green Party activist, none of these people had engaged in political activism very much beforehand, although they mostly profess a left-of-centre politics. They had largely sat out the referendum campaign, but their strong feelings about the result compelled them to action. Setting up groups, running street stalls, attending protests and writing to politicians, they would all spend significant portions of the next years of their lives engaged in grassroots pro-European activism. These people and people like them would form the engine and often set the tone of the anti-Brexit and pro-second referendum movements. They were what made these efforts not just political campaigns, but a genuine grassroots social movement.

Like them, Tom Brufatto was, by his own account, 'not involved in politics' before the referendum, although he had become a Labour member after Cameron had won the election. He was starting his career, working at Rolls-Royce as an aeronautical engineer (he advises me to say aeronautical instead of just engineer; otherwise, apparently, people think of cars) and living in Bristol. In the last week of the referendum campaign he'd delivered some leaflets with Labour In because he'd been worried about the outcome. When the result was as he'd feared, he decided to get active and did so in a very 2016 way: he started a Facebook page and called it 'Bristol for Europe'. He remembers that 'in days it had reached a thousand or so members'.

Brufatto recalls a pretty 'tumultuous' pro-European scene in the immediate aftermath of the referendum. He drove to

London for an early protest in Parliament Square, but 'there really weren't that many of us there'. There were a lot of people trying to get things going in the post-Brexit, anti-Brexit space, but nothing was really sticking:

> There was something called Project Remain for a while, which lasted for a short period, then there was March for Europe, which was a protest group that was run by one of the founders of Secret Cinema that lasted for a short period of time, just to name a few.

He connected offline with some people from his Facebook group: 'We decided to formalise the group, set it up, and Bristol for Europe grew from there and I became its chair'. Soon, he connected with people in London and ended up as chair of a national umbrella organisation for local groups like his. It was called 'Britain for Europe'.

Around the country, others were thinking and doing along similar lines, many coming into contact with Britain for Europe as they did so. Wancke and Brown were among those who founded North East for Europe; Richard Wilson became chair of Leeds for Europe. Maggie Turner, the inventor of the bEUret, became active in Bath for Europe. In December of 2016, Gordon found his way to his first meeting of Oxford for Europe, with three or four people in a busy pub in St Clement's. He tells me his 'first assignment' as a newly minted activist was to 'go to Leeds for a joint meeting of the embryonic affiliated groups of Britain for Europe'. He had also joined Facebook for the first time after the referendum result and was beginning to 'fight the good fight' online, joining pro-European groups like 'The 48%', a group where many of the activists profiled here would hang out, organising, setting the world to rights and 'arguing with trolls'.

Abroad, Sue Wilson (no relation to Richard) was soon heavily involved in running Bremain in Spain, which came to work closely with Britain for Europe. She quickly became chair, and estimates that in the years after the referendum, she spent about seventy hours a week on running Bremain in Spain, working seven days a week. One person working in the space remembers receiving daily press releases from her, which they described as 'terrible press strategy', evincing a 'total misunderstanding of how the media works' but nonetheless 'actually quite effective and impressive in its own wide-eyed kind of way'.

Beyond 'people similarly horrified and activated by Brexit', it is worth spending a bit of time thinking about who the people involved in these nascent anti-Brexit movements actually were. For the full picture on this, you are best off reading *The Failure of Remain*, by political scientists Stijn van Kessel and Adam Fagan. Their book focuses itself on understanding the grassroots anti-Brexit movement by, among other things, conducting a study of participants. One of the more revealing statistics in the book is a demographic look at who those participants were. Of those they surveyed, 87 per cent were forty-five and older and 41 per cent were sixty-five or older. Some 58 per cent of them had a postgraduate qualification and fewer than 10 per cent finished formal education at eighteen or younger.[1]

In short, they are old and they are middle class. They probably went to university at a time when far, far fewer people did than do today. This fits with the general perception of the pro-European movement in the media and in general discussion. It also fits with the impressions I gathered in researching this book and with the view that those I interviewed had about the demographics of their own movement. Asked about who made up the base of his Leeds for Europe group, Richard Wilson said 'middle-class people, well-educated' people. One Lincolnshire for Europe activist told Fagan and van Kessel that there was 'a tendency for it to look very white and very middle class', while someone active in the European Movement dubbed it 'pale, male and stale'.[2]

While speaking with Adam Fagan, who is in his fifties and a professor of European politics at King's College London, he remarked that one of the things that had really struck him when interviewing activists was that they were almost all 'my age and older'. Part, I suspect, of the reason why Brufatto came to be the one running Britain for Europe is that he was fairly young and vital. In the land of the pensioner, the 26-year-old man is king – this is a dynamic which, thanks to the anti-Brexit movement's odd relationship with young people and youth campaigners, we will see recurring throughout the book.

Fagan and van Kessel spend some time comparing the anti-Brexit protest movement to groups on the continent, such as the pro-EU federalist group Volt, but in truth, these groups had little precedent in the UK. Anand Menon remembers 'thinking it was very ironic' that 'it took us leaving for us to develop a pro-European grassroots movement, which we'd never really had when we were in the EU'.

The quip that comes up again and again in these discussions about the demographics of the activists who made up the anti-Brexit campaign is the assertion that the big London protests that would come in 2018 and 2019 looked like 'the longest Waitrose queue in history'. This is, obviously, a pejorative assessment, but taking it as the assessment of class and age it is meant as, it is one which is broadly borne out. I would also hazard that it would be likely further borne out by more studies.

The rejoinder to this is that, in fact, the demographics of people who actively do politics in the UK are, well, disproportionately old and middle class. It's not a Remainer problem, you might argue: it's a Labour problem, a Tory problem, a politics problem. It's a fair observation, but I would argue it doesn't entirely take the edge off the demographics at play in the Remainer grassroots. We are, after all, not talking about strict party politics; we're talking about a protest movement. There is also a degree of self-direction at play in the pro-European grassroots. Similar demographics appear within, say, the Labour Party too, but within other structures they are not so self-directing because they are intercut and diluted by a range of other factors. Its independence makes the anti-Brexit social movement, I believe, the purer ID of the liberal middle classes.

Real though it is, you can overstretch and overread this

demographic reality; it's possible to use it to project onto the entire movement an air of elitism and inauthenticity, to what I would consider an ultimately misleading end. But just as you shouldn't overread it, it is foolish to try to minimise or deny that the demographic make-up of the grassroots of the anti-Brexit movement was a certain way and that meant that it wanted certain things, had certain concerns and acted in certain ways.

Moving from demographics to motivation, a further thing binding together these grassroots activists was their strength of feeling about Brexit and about Europe. Almost everyone we will encounter in this book, from the people running North East for Europe to the politicians, advisers and New Labour doyennes we will meet in later chapters, feels bad, upset and angry about Brexit. The observation that people experienced Brexit more emotionally than other political events is not a novel one, nor indeed is the idea that the referendum, as *The Politics of Feeling in Brexit Britain* describes, 'ushered in an unusually emotional moment in national life'.[3]

However, for all that the trope of the 'angry Brexiteer and the rational/grieving Remainer' is one we all recognise – backing up the fact that 'in public discourse on the EU referendum, Leave was invariably cast as the emotional choice and Remain the rational one' – in their study of feelings about Brexit from the Mass Observation archive, Jonathan Moss, Emily Robinson and Jake Watts found that 'Remainers were as likely to emphasise their emotional investments in the topic' as Leavers.[4] In his 2018 survey of Leave and Remain identification,

John Curtice wrote that while 'there has been some tendency among those who would like the UK to remain in the EU to suggest that many Leave voters' support for exiting the EU is based more on emotional considerations than on any rational evaluation of what is in Britain's best interests,' in actuality,

> those who say they would now vote Leave in another EU referendum are only slightly more likely to identify as a Leaver (92 per cent) than those who would back Remain are to identify as a Remainer (89 per cent). Meanwhile, those who identify as a Remainer are actually more likely than those who say they are a Leaver to declare that their attachment is 'very strong'.[5]

It is here, among the local groups, the retirees who showed up week in and week out and the wearers of the bEUrets, I think, that those emotional investments are most intense; this is the kingdom of the 'very strong' Remainer. There is also reason to suspect that this level of emotional involvement stood in the way of good political process over Brexit. Many political scientists, reasonably, consider the idea of 'losers' consent' to be essential 'for democracies to govern effectively'.[6] That is, people who didn't get their way still have to accept the result. However, the emotional intensity and polarisation that surrounded Brexit, the academics James Tilley and Sara Hobolt have argued, can be understood to have acted upon the level of losers' consent available surrounding the vote.[7] This can, then, be understood to have had an adverse impact on the polity's overall handling of the situation.

Where were people getting all this feeling and identity from, in their own telling of it? A great many of the people I spoke to talked about having travelled in Europe in their youth. Brown remembers learning about the benefits of the EU while at a 'rough school' in Sunderland and going on to study languages and do an Erasmus programme. Wancke recalls busking on the Continent in her twenties, meeting 'such brilliant people', while Gordon says that 'all my life has been mixed up with Europe one way or another'. An expert in the philosopher Michel Foucault, when he was a PhD student in Oxford in the 1970s, he went over for a term to Paris and ended up as one of Foucault's translators, having previously spent a period living and working in Germany.

Personal contact with Michel Foucault notwithstanding, these are not unusual stories. Fagan tells me that many of the activists he spoke to had told him 'very similar stories' of time abroad. 'They'd gone interrailing or they'd studied abroad … they'd done something at a time, perhaps, when travel wasn't as easy,' and as a result had become 'really infatuated with Europe and with languages and culture.' These experiences and infatuation had led to a 'very strong emotional attachment … which was forged in their youth and it was very much part of their personal narrative.' This feeling was 'very strongly connected to identity' and how they thought of themselves and the country – and the wider world – in which they lived. Many of them, Fagan says, 'use the language of trauma' to talk about the result.

This point is vital to understanding just what so intensely

animated the anti-Brexit grassroots. 'I do think a class and an age of person felt like their identity had been trashed by what happened,' one person who worked on the later second referendum campaign told me. When people feel that their self-conception has been traduced and invalidated – at scale, by a national referendum, no less – they are going to be extremely exercised about it. While a lot of what they were technically protesting involved anger on behalf of freedoms lost by future generations, particularly the freedom to work and travel, the sense one gets from talking to a sufficiently large number of people who became activists is not that they were out on the streets because their children's or grandchildren's future had been stolen or trespassed against so much as their own youth had been.

'I think it's something that people still don't quite get, that those identity issues are so crucial,' says Menon. 'There was an emotional attachment to the idea of Europe and European integration that went beyond "this is good for our economy". It was matters of "I feel European". I think that was a very, very key part of it.' While there were obviously economic and other concerns motivating the anti Brexit campaigners, to Menon's view a core motivation is one that is 'more abstract', concerned with a 'vision of the UK's place in the world, a vision of our identity as being as European as we were British. And of course, that's not something that everyone shares.' As such, 'it's quite hard to persuade people' arguing from that perspective.

It is also worth thinking about what it meant for the

grassroots that it was made up, by and large, of political neophytes, as this would fuel tensions with other parts of the movement throughout the campaign. Fagan says that his interest in the grassroots was first piqued when attending some of the marches himself: he was struck by the 'localism' and the 'amateur' nature of what he saw. You can, if you are sufficiently interested in this subject as to be reading this book, likely summon to mind what he's referring to: handmade signs and EU flags, banners for dozens upon dozens of small local groups and generally less presence from the larger organisations – unions, charities, campaign groups, political parties – than you might expect from a political march of a similar size.

This newly forged interest in politics had its upsides – dedication and vibrancy, an interest in art and culture – but it also had its downsides, such as evincing, as discussed, a 'total misunderstanding of how the media works' or lacking a thoroughgoing understanding of how to effect political change in the UK. What political experience they did have was generally not applicable to the particular persuasion challenges of getting a new referendum. One grassroots activist I spoke to describes herself as a 'centrist and lefty' but not a member of any party. Active in her local area, she had spent twenty years fighting 'a plan by the Tory town council here to develop a rewilded allotment site into housing. This involved a lot of work, including starting a local residents' group.'

One People's Vote staffer I spoke to said, 'Some of the people who were, for the first time, really motivated by this, this was the first major injustice in their life,' adding that there was an element of not quite understanding what impacts their actions could or would reasonably have on the government.

He explains:

> You'd go to Cheltenham or some place like that – and actually, they're pretty much all places the Lib Dems have done well in recently – and they're people who are actually quite well off ... that doesn't make their concerns any less valid. You're obviously entitled to have a strong opinion about the way the country makes this major decision. But I think it's a really interesting fact that it meant that people came and thought that they could turn up to a million-person march and obviously the government would listen, and [they] sort of hadn't had that interaction before.

That interaction being one where, actually, it is unlikely that the government will listen and unlikelier still that any action will be taken. One Labour member involved struck a similar note. 'For many people in the votes-Blair, votes-Cameron demographic, it was the first time they had been on the losing side politically,' they said, likening it to 'stages of grief':

> But the reason it was so much harder for them to work through the stages of grief is because, unlike many of us in Labour, unlike people from most other bits of politics, the group of people that make up the demographic, they hadn't had to go

through the stages of grief politically as often as many of the rest of us.

One activist interviewed by van Kessel and Fagan relayed a frustration with fellow volunteers who 'want to stand on a street corner, wrapping themselves in an EU flag, shouting to everyone "how much I love the EU" and telling people [that] factually, they are incorrect'. This is not, of course, effective messaging or canvassing. While this may not have been at all the majority view or behaviour of activists, it is hard (as many people interviewed in this book expressed) to impose message discipline on large numbers of impassioned people giving up their time for free, organised across many disparate groups. Unfortunately, it can be hard to avoid being seen through the prism of one's silliest members.

Britain for Europe built steam through the end of 2016 and through 2017. Street stalls were a big part of the different groups' activities. Richard Wilson remembers doing them in Leeds 'every week for quite a long period of time, for a couple of years, really'. He also remembers just generally trying to amp up the group's activity: holding 'public meetings, increasing social media' and getting letters and articles into the newspapers.

One woman active in her local European Movement chapter remembers the group as being 'a fairly good mix of ages and political persuasions, from Greens to Tory voters, although much like the general Remain community, I'd say most were white, middle class and centrist.' She notes that she 'was the youngest at twenty-nine'. Their group were particularly keen on street stalls: 'Most groups' street stalls seemed to last only a couple of hours, but ours could last anything up to seven or eight hours – we were very keen.' However, the conversations were, she recalls, not always helpful.

> There's no polite way to say it, we regularly met a lot of not very bright people who didn't talk much sense – 'I voted Leave because [town]'s market's not what it used to be, it's all hair extensions now' – and so it wasn't really possible to get anywhere with them. But mostly the people we spoke to were just sick of hearing about Brexit.

She added that doing the stalls was not always a pleasant experience. There would sometimes be 'aggressive men of all ages, a few of whom screamed and shouted in my face, which is not something I experienced with other kinds of public-facing activism'.

On street stalls, 'Brexitometers' – 'a whiteboard with statements about Brexit on which passersby could indicate their (dis)agreement by means of colourful stickers' – were popular props, Fagan and van Kessel write. This was particularly the case given that 'responses overwhelmingly skewed against Brexit, which provided good material for social media posts featuring images of the Brexitometers'.[8] People I spoke to generally referred to them as conversation starters, something to draw people in so they could have a discussion, productive or otherwise.

In the period we're currently discussing, the reasonably immediate aftermath of the referendum, the call for a second referendum was not yet what these groups were asking for or oriented towards. Britain for Europe's slogan was, Brufatto remembers, 'simply "Stop Brexit"'. As Wancke explains, 'What we really wanted was to reverse Brexit. At that point, it wasn't about a second referendum … it was that we've made the most terrible, terrible mistake and it needs to be changed, and at that point, that was the campaign.'

Britain for Europe had affiliated, fairly smoothly, to the pre-existing European Movement via a vote of chairs of local groups. This made sense; the European Movement had history. It had been founded in the late 1940s and its first president had been the Conservative MP, and Churchill's son-in-law, Duncan Sandys. It did have a local group structure, but by the time of the referendum it was 'largely dormant', with its local groups little more than 'wine and cheese clubs'.[9] There were only around 700 members nationally, organised into roughly fifteen local chapters.[10] Affiliation could give the new groups legitimacy and the European Movement vitality, with neither demanding very much of the other. Along with convenience, there was also an ideological compatibility.

Brendan Donnelly was, at the time of the referendum and in the years following, treasurer of the European Movement, a position he tells me he had held since around '2008 or 2009', having been involved since the 1990s. His entire career has been dedicated to the European project; after graduating from university in the early 1970s, he spent time working for the Foreign Office in Germany ('I found that was a very, very successful exercise in state building, a very attractive one. And it seemed to me to be that the European Union was at the centre of modern German identity'). However, he rebukes me for suggesting that these positive experiences abroad played a part in his broader political commitment: 'You almost hint that it would be so eccentric for somebody to think positively about Europe that they had to have lived in Germany, or there must be some specific reason for that.' He then relented and agreed that this was 'part of it', alongside an ideological commitment to European integration and 'because I find English nationalism so tedious'. He apologises for rebuking me: 'Sorry, I'm feeling rather querulous. I just had a number of very, very unappreciative tweets coming back to me from what I thought were some good tweets.'

By the 1980s, Donnelly was working for the Conservative group of MEPs in Brussels. 'In those days, the Conservative Party was, of the two main parties, much more pro-European,' he explains. In the 1990s, he became a Conservative MEP himself. He split from the party in 1999 to found the 'Pro-Euro Conservative Party' and was not re-elected, whereupon he briefly joined the Liberal Democrats but 'didn't particularly feel at home there'. He stood for two further pro-European parties (unsuccessfully) and is currently the director of the Federal Trust and leader of the Rejoin EU Party, which will be discussed further in Chapter 15.

He remembers that after the referendum, some in the European Movement took the position that they had to 'accept it. We've just got to live with it; perhaps at some point we can advocate being in the single market.' However,

> the majority view, in which I participated and spoke in favour [of], was that in a democracy, people are perfectly entitled to change their minds, and the European Movement should be committed to reversing Brexit. And I couldn't see the point of a European Movement – this was a view shared by many – unless it was committed to reversing Brexit.

This majority position was simpatico with the view in the new Britain for Europe groups, and so the European Movement became the home of grassroots anti-Brexit activism.

However, the simple (and admittedly somewhat unlikely) animating goal of just stopping Brexit, held by Britain for Europe and the European Movement, would, in the time after the 2017 election, be overtaken by a new ask, with a new infrastructure growing up around it: the call for a second referendum. But by this point, many in Britain for Europe and similar grassroots organisations had been at it for more than a year, organising themselves, writing to MPs and marching in the streets. They were not sure they wanted to adopt a new demand, especially one which, even if it came to fruition, might not stop Brexit. After all, people could still vote no at that referendum too.

Richard Wilson's 'early reaction' was that 'this is a big problem that we have in the country, and a technical fix isn't going to be enough'. There needed to be a 'big debate in this country' and progressives needed to 'defeat these ideas that have taken hold, which are really quite unpleasant and dangerous ideas'. Wancke 'wasn't very keen on it initially, because I didn't really want a referendum. I still don't really want a referendum, because I think referendums are terrible ways to run a country.'

Hesitancy over the second-referendum strategy, coupled with a suspicion of top-down control carrying over from the original Stronger In campaign, made throwing Britain for Europe's lot in with the People's Vote campaign, when it formed in early 2018, not as straightforward a call as joining up with the European Movement. By that point, Brufatto estimates, they had around 'a hundred local activist groups, many of them with thousands of supporters in them. We probably had roughly one hundred thousand people in the local groups, in a decentralised structure that was very bottom-up as opposed to top-down.' As chair, he was firmly of the view that joining up would be a good next move for the organisation. 'I spent quite a bit of time with the more sceptical local groups and activists in Britain for Europe to try and get us there,' he tells me.

When the organisation agreed on this course of action, Brufatto quit his job – being chair of Britain for Europe had, until then, been an entirely voluntary role – and moved to London to begin work as a full-time anti-Brexit agitator. In keeping with his grassroots connections and experience, he recalls that his responsibilities were 'supporting and developing the local groups and organising the marches'. It would not prove to be a smooth ride.

CHAPTER 2

THE INFLUENCERS

At the time of the Brexit referendum, Madeleina Kay was a student living in Sheffield and studying for a degree in landscape architecture. She'd voted Green and been a member of the Lib Dems but wasn't hugely politically active. 'I'd made some posts on Facebook in response to Nigel Farage's "Breaking Point" poster,' she says, but that was about it.

However, like pretty much everyone else in this book, she was horrified by the result of the referendum ('it really made no sense to me, the way people voted'), which she said 'triggered something in me, like an emotional reaction'. Kay channelled this into art, beginning to write songs and putting together a children's picture book ('it was trying to tell the story of a refugee, but through animal characters'), which she then published through a crowdfunding campaign. The book was a surprise success. She sold them in aid of a local refugee group, bringing in around £1,800, which, Kay says, 'brought me a lot of traction'. She was asked by the Sheffield Lib Dems to perform at a rally, then by North East for Europe and then by a slew of local groups that had sprung up or been rejuvenated in the aftermath of the vote.

> I was just getting endless requests … can you make a cartoon about this? Can you design this? We want to put an ad van around London. Can you design a propagandist image for the side of the ad van? Can you perform at this rally we're organising? And it just snowballed from there.

She dropped out of her course at the end of 2016 (she'd never been that keen on landscape architecture anyway, she says) and became a full-time pro-EU campaigner: 'It took over my life, it was ridiculous.' As the journalist Daniel Cohen describes it, her 'cult following was boosted by the music videos she posted online,' which he characterises as 'occupying the naffer edges of Remainism … the kind of love songs or break-up ballads one might hear at an open-mic night, but addressed to the EU ('always thought you were the problem, now I see the problem was me').'[1]

She started attending anti-Brexit marches; at the first one she went to, her first-ever demo, she put a T-shirt on her dog. 'Everybody was taking photos of the dog; people were obsessed with the dog. And it made me realise – they want a visual image to illustrate the campaign narrative.' After that she began to dress up, too. At the next march she went to, the organiser spotted her: 'Oh, young woman, cool dog, all in blue. Yeah, you're walking at the front with Eddie Izzard and Peter Tatchell.'

Kay realised that she could get attention and traction from colourful costumes and placards. Her first costume was, she says, a pirate: 'That was when the right-wing press were calling us saboteurs, sabotaging Brexit … I thought, I'll make a pirate costume and have "proud saboteur" on it.' But it was at an anti-Brexit march in Manchester in 2017 that she first stepped out in a Supergirl costume. It was pretty low effort: 'I just bought a Supergirl outfit and then sewed stars on.'

'What happened was I entered this competition. It was a blogging competition organised by the European Commission, called "EU in my region", and I'd written about a landscape architecture scheme in Sheffield,' Kay says. She won, 'and the prize was to go to Brussels, and they gave us some training on journalism and gave us a press pass so that we could attend press events associated with the EU regions week.' Kay was tipped off that the Brexit negotiations press conference was going on while she was in town. The person who tipped her off also signed her into the Berlaymont building where the conference was happening, where, because of her press pass, she could move about freely and attend press conferences (but was not allowed to ask questions).

> After getting into the building, I went to the toilets and put on my Supergirl costume and went into the press conference and just sat on the front row. I didn't say anything; I didn't do anything. I just sat there in this costume and the other media outlets that were there just went mental. I think there was a photo that appeared on the *Guardian* live stream of the back

> of my head on the front row and just all of these, like a wall of cameras of just everybody trying to interview me.

The press conference had been to discuss the latest developments in the Brexit talks and was to feature David Davis and Michel Barnier, but Kay became the main event. 'EU Supergirl causes more of a stir than Davis and Barnier pre-#Brexit press conference,' tweeted one journalist.[2] Kay, holding a copy of her children's book *Theresa Maybe in Brexitland* (she says she has self-published nine books as of 2024), was escorted out of the press conference and received widespread media attention.

And so, in a slew of headlines and articles, EU Supergirl was born – somewhat to Kay's chagrin:

> They gave me the name EU Supergirl. I didn't give it to myself, and they started using the hashtag 'EU Supergirl'. It's not something that I invented. I mean, obviously I wore the costume, yeah, but I hadn't been going around calling myself the Supergirl … I did loads of other costumes afterwards. I did a Wonder Woman costume. I did a sailor. I've done loads of costumes, but it was always the EU Supergirl one that just stuck.

With this, she gained a degree of very specific fame, joining the ranks of the pro-EU micro-celebrities. Through the end of 2016 and into 2017, the grassroots anti-Brexit movement, the people we met in Chapter 1, had grown, both in terms of their online and their real-world presence. Having become a world unto themselves, the grassroots was able to support a handful of full-time influencers (who one could also term protesters, or activists or, if feeling uncharitable, grifters). I believe that these people should be understood as a function of the grassroots. If the Britain for Europe and European Movement groups could be understood as the id of a certain part of Britain's middle class, these people were their mascots. 'You didn't really have to dig that far' into the world of hardcore pro-Europeanism, anti-Brexit campaigner Amanda Chetwynd-Cowieson remembers, 'to come across these almost like, inner-world celebs'.

Outside of the movement itself, these people often could have a degree of purchase on the broader, not quite so hardcore Remain constituency – the *Guardian*- and *Independent*-reading people who weren't among Tom Brufatto's estimated 100,000 activists but would be in the crowd for the marches of 700,000 or more later in the campaign. As Kay had learned, the press was keen for images to illustrate Brexit stories; people saw her photograph or saw her on social media, and her very specific fame grew. Kay, in her role as a quasi-public figure, had a fairly clear idea of what her role was: winning hearts and minds.

Kay was unambiguously anti-Brexit but thought another referendum was the way to overturn the decision: 'My ambition was always stopping Brexit before it happened. But I knew that the only way that that could or should be done was through a second referendum.' She had fairly mixed views on the formal campaign to get a new referendum, however.

> If you invest all your energy, as the People's Vote campaign did, all the energy, resources, money, into just getting a second referendum and pretending that you're impartial and putting no effort into changing public opinion, it's a high-risk strategy, because you could not get a referendum, which is what happened. And then all of that time, money, resources were wasted and public opinion hasn't changed either. Whereas, if you put the effort into changing public opinion and you don't get the referendum, OK, Brexit goes ahead, but you've laid the groundwork for taking us back into the EU in the long run. That was my thinking. So, all of my effort was [put] into trying to change public perception of the EU.

Kay, in movement terms – along with Femi Oluwole and Steve Bray, aka the Stop Brexit Man, both of whom we will be meeting in subsequent chapters – was about as famous as it was possible to be. But, as in any ecosystem, there were layers of fame; there were only a smattering of full-time influencers but plenty of part-time ones.

Sarah Jones became known as, as she puts it, 'a minor Remain celebrity' under the pseudonym 'Sarah Saboteur'. As with Kay's pirate costume, the name was playing on the infamous April 2017 *Daily Mail* front page that featured an image of Theresa May with the headline 'Crush the Saboteurs'. She 'quickly gained thousands of Twitter followers from scratch'. Soon, it spilled over into the real world; she even 'started getting recognised on the street and having strangers approach me asking to take a selfie with me'. She recalls, 'My "fame" also led to me being asked to give interviews to local and international media, and I was invited to film an interview for *Channel 4 News* about the effects of Brexit on mental health.'

Jones is clearly faintly baffled by this, saying that while she hasn't done much political activism, 'I don't think that's typical of most political campaigns, where random people can get catapulted into pseudo-celebrity status overnight like a reality TV show.'

Jones speculates via email interview that there was 'something quite different about the Remain campaign, perhaps because the online community was so emotionally invested in it (due to Brexit being such an emotive topic?) and increasingly desperate for leadership, so they leapt on anyone they could follow, both as a leader and a social media figure'. Ed Shackle, who spent time working for anti-Brexit youth organisation Our Future Our Choice, reflected on this as well. 'You put out a tweet, and you would get thousands of likes,' he recalls. 'There was a real sense [that] there was a percentage of the country who were very intensely interested in what you're doing. And I think that sort of grew these personalities quite quickly.' You could 'balloon' online, says Shackle, as Jones did. He reckons, 'It was a good time to go viral.'

Jones felt somewhat obligated to make use of the platform that had suddenly grown up underneath her, and she would post videos and other content 'encouraging others and explaining how to find their own nearest pro-EU groups, how to run a street stall and collect petition signatures'. However, she says, 'I found it quite frustrating how many "likes" I would get when I was posting live updates from the street stalls and trying to recruit other activists, compared to how many people actually got actively involved.' She goes on: 'There were a fair number of people who took the whole campaign very seriously but spent most of their time sat online obsessing over "Remain celebrities", including random nobodies like me, and bickering among themselves, rather than doing anything helpful.'

This insularity is a key part of understanding both the grassroots and their influencer class; as the journalist Daniel Cohen argued in 2019, a lot of hardcore Remainers weren't 'actually very interested in Leavers. They prefer to look inward, at the 48% rather than the 52%. Surrounded by people who get their jokes, they have finally found a political identity that fits them. That means their priority is mobilising opinion, not changing it.'[3]

Living in this inner world, even only as a part-time influencer, took up a lot of time. Jones says that between her involvement in her local European Movement group (she designed and ordered their leaflets) and keeping the Sarah Saboteur persona running, anti-Brexit activism ended up taking up 'as much of my time as a heavy part-time job would'.

If it was a new job to some in the space, to others it was simply an adaptation of what they'd been doing all along, among them Drew Galdron. Galdron has been impersonating Boris Johnson for almost fifteen years. They signed with a lookalike agency in 2011 and by the time of the referendum, they tell me, 'I had already been impersonating Boris Johnson professionally for nearly five years.'

On the night of the referendum, Galdron was working: 'I was hired for a party near Oxford Circus alongside a David Cameron lookalike.' Galdron had an Out rosette and fake Cameron had an In rosette (the reverse of the two lookalikes' actual votes, I'm told), and the pair were greeting guests and being generally entertaining at what Galdron remembers as a 'casino night-themed party for a law firm'.

Despite, unsurprisingly, looking and sounding strikingly like Boris Johnson (speaking to them via Zoom from my flat, my partner in the next room assumed that I was listening to clips of Johnson speaking), Galdron professes quite different politics to the former Prime Minister. 'I now call myself a queer anarchist,' they tell me, while acknowledging that those are 'utopian politics'. 'My realistic politics are closer to progressive liberal,' they acknowledge. They didn't vote for Boris when he stood to be Mayor of London in 2008, instead opting for Green and putting Labour second, and were firmly opposed to Brexit, viewing it as the final manifestation of a 'culture that had become obsessed with fear'.

After the referendum, Galdron became involved with a group that started to call itself the Downing Street Vigil, who would meet at Downing Street to protest and mourn Brexit. 'We eventually put on a puppet show ahead of the 2017 election,' they tell me. Interestingly, hardcore Remain puppetry seems to be a bit of a thing. At the 2024 Rejoin March, I briefly interviewed the host of *The Strange Mole Show*, an anti-Brexit podcast, who spoke to me in part through his ventriloquist's dummy (no, I'm not sure how that works in an audio-only format either).

Galdron's involvement in anti-Brexit campaigning only grew, and by 'May or June 2018' they had moved to south London and were 'living in the same flat as Steve Bray'. Galdron 'was there specifically to be on standby for any stunts'; the owner of the flat was another activist 'of somewhat better means than the rest of us' who 'was prepared to let us stay there for free' and 'wanted it to be a stop-off for any other activists'.

There were some tensions in the anti-Brexit hype house, where Kay would also sometimes stay while doing stunts and performing in London, but 'most of the time we got along OK,' Galdron remembers. Galdron lived there for about a year and a half, while 'Steve was eventually, in 2019, keeping a lot of his things in that same flat but also staying at an Airbnb in Westminster to keep even closer to the action'.

Being so intensely involved in anti-Brexit activism, Galdron remembers, 'My mental health took a real hit, because I guess it felt as though Brexit was like this looming darkness and then obviously the dread that we couldn't stop it.' Boris Johnson becoming Prime Minister also sparked feelings of dread for Galdron, but

> on the outside, I had to try and convey this confident image, like I could be him or I could at least overcome his lies as his conscience. That was another big part of the image of me at a

lot of these protests and stunts, that I was the conscience of Boris Johnson.

Performing parody songs was one of the regular things Galdron did at protests and other events. In their repertoire was a version of 'No Good Deed' from *Wicked* (it's 'a song that's not in the movie, because the movie is only the first part of the musical,' Galdron patiently explains to me, a person who has seen neither of the films nor the stage musical). 'I rewrote that into it being about Boris singing "no good cleave goes unpunished", and it was … the mirror of him divorcing Marina Wheeler with the divorce of Britain from the EU,' Galdron explains.

In December 2018, Galdron, Kay and others from the EU Flag Mafia group travelled the country (and even did international stops in Dublin and Brussels) on the 'Bollocks to Brexit Bus Tour'. The bus visited Theresa May's Maidenhead constituency and Corbyn's Islington North patch. Kay remembers debate about whether they would use the word 'bollocks' up front, lest 'broadcasters would use that as an excuse not to give any publicity'. However, the side that ultimately won the argument asserted, she remembers, that 'our campaign movement love this message, it's chanted at every single march and event,' and as such, 'the only way we're going to crowdfund the money to do the tour is if this is the message that we put on it'. This story neatly demonstrates the ratchet present throughout the second referendum movement: moderating a message might give it more popular reach (and indeed appeal), but it's the base that pays the bills and, ultimately, money talks.

As they functioned in tandem with the grassroots, the demographic problems discussed in Chapter 1 were relevant here as well. 'The grassroots activists tended to be old white people,' remembers Kay,

> and I think this was one of the reasons why I gained such a profile within the movement, because there were not very many young people and particularly not very many young women. I think that contributed to the fact that I was getting asked to speak or perform at so many events, because it's like, 'Oh God, we've got a panel of all old white men, no diversity. Oh, look, there's a young person and a woman.' So, there's our token representation.

Kay also reckons that 'for sure, the people that were donating to my crowdfunders were older, white, well-educated people, because they had the disposable income and they were the ones that were engaged with the campaign'.

With their obscenity buses, their music of dubious quality and their blue and yellow outfits, the influencers were not viewed as universally helpful to the anti-Brexit cause. 'I bet most people would say Madeleina was unhelpful,' Sarah Jones says, 'not the centrist dads, obviously.' (Jones here alludes to the perception that Kay particularly attracted the gaze and support of a particular kind of middle-aged man who was angry about Britain leaving the European Union.)

But, Jones says, while she 'didn't agree with some of her techniques', Kay's

> colourful approach gave the media something to cover. Why would they bother writing an article about a bunch of old fogeys shuffling around moaning about the EU referendum? But when she turned up with her costumes and her guitar, suddenly they had a story and some photos to print and the campaign got coverage – it didn't so much matter if it was positive or negative, because it made people aware that there was a growing movement protesting Brexit and wanting the deal put to a confirmatory referendum and that was enough.

Tom Baldwin, director of communications at the People's Vote campaign, from whom we will hear much more in future chapters, clearly takes a fairly dim view on the more exuberant elements of the grassroots and what we might understand as their influencer class. 'The clue should have been in the title,' he says:

> We were the People's Vote campaign, not the campaign to persuade more people to love Europe. With the best will in the world, someone dressing up in a blue flag and yellow stars to sing bad songs about the glories of the European project was unlikely to convince a wavering Tory or Labour MP to support us.

In his view, their activities weren't about 'getting politics done' but rather 'about asserting an identity'.

Others took a harsher view still. 'It felt a bit at the time like we were being hijacked by opportunists,' one People's Vote staffer said.

> People like Madeleina Kay would come in and jump in the front of this highly curated event where Jo Johnson was speaking with Gary Lineker. She would stand up on stage, not part of it, and then suddenly the images that come out of it are someone draped with an EU flag and it's undone the sensible approach.

The staffer here is specifically referring to Kay's appearance at a November 2018 event held in Methodist Central Hall in Westminster.

As one member of the People's Vote's comms team told me, 'Celebs in the EU world… their message discipline was perhaps not…' The staffer reached for a moderated term, unsuccessfully, before concluding that 'the way in which they got their support was often being very pro-EU and that didn't necessarily align with the campaign generally'.

'At the very least,' says Richard Brooks, who founded a youth anti-Brexit group,

> I think [niche anti-Brexit micro-celebrities] were wrapping up a lot of their self-interest in what they would suggest was the wider goals of the movement. And I don't think that's fair. And at worst, were, you know, just using the goodwill of people who care about Brexit to basically give themselves a profile.

However, Galdron takes an even dimmer view of Baldwin et al. than they take of Galdron et al. 'I think we've all, most of us, ended up having to take the view, in hindsight, that the People's Vote were not what they seemed,' says Galdron.

> They were almost a sabotage operation in themselves … if they weren't directing away from simply criticising Brexit, away from straightforward criticism of it, then they were at least putting a corporate sanitised face on a second referendum campaign, which then deliberately was going to make it less good.

'There were accusations that they may have been infiltrated by Brexit fifth colonists,' they conclude, expressing (more directly than most) a sentiment I heard a few times across my interviews for this book. This conspiratorial thinking put me in mind of a quote from political scientist Rob Ford, who, in discussing hardcore Remainers, remarked that much of their reasoning was to him 'just so reminiscent of how radical-right voters would think'.[4]

CHAPTER 3

THE MEDIA

Just as the grassroots and the wider surge of anti-Brexit sentiment could support a layer of influencers, so too could they support a media ecosystem of their own. What Daniel Cohen termed the Remainists were a valuable market segment – people sick of what they saw as cack-handed attempts at balance when it came to what they viewed as a grievous act of national self-harm. They wanted news by and for the 48 per cent; less charitably, you might say that they wanted to talk to themselves. This again comes back to the strength of feeling among strong Remainers discussed in the last chapter. As Tilley and Hobolt put it, 'Angry people consume less countervailing political information and are more likely to support emotionally framed political positions.'[1] And the Remainers were certainly angry.

Perhaps surprisingly, given how much of the anti-Brexit moment was happening online, in the recesses of heaving Facebook groups and at the bottom of Twitter feeds, one of the quickest off the mark was a good old-fashioned weekly newspaper.

Matt Kelly had been working as chief content officer at the

media company Archant, which owned a range of local newspapers, for about six months when the referendum happened. He hadn't really engaged with the vote and had been 'as complacent as anyone' beforehand, but says that when the result came through 'the shock of the consequences started to really, really dawn on me'.

Kelly remembers talking to his boss at Archant that day and saying,

> If ever there was a time for a new newspaper it's right now, because you've got this group of people who didn't exist yesterday – the 48 per cent. They've got a name; they're pissed off that nobody represents them properly in the media. They're all galvanised by this issue. We know where they are geographically: you know exactly where the Remain areas are versus the Leave areas. And there's a whole new constituency of people that are ripe for a new publication.

He thought there was a gap in the market for not just an informative bit of media but a marker of identity.

> If you think about how can you visibly demonstrate your alignment with a set of policies or a particular political party, it's actually quite hard when it comes down to it. You can wear a badge, you can paint a placard, you can go on a march or you can buy a newspaper. You can read a newspaper and say this is who I'm interested in; this is who I am.

Kelly, speaking to me in early 2025, was here reiterating a point he made when talking about the paper's launch to *The Guardian* in 2016, where he said that he believed people would 'read and carry' the paper as a 'badge of honour'.[2]

Kelly's boss was interested in the idea. At their next meeting, which Kelly remembers as primarily being 'this very gloomy diagnostic of the consequences of Brexit, right down to things like the cost of importing newspaper paper and ink', the proposed new paper was given the go-ahead. The only concerns raised were financial. Kelly says the recent and disastrous failure of the Trinity Mirror group's newspaper the *New Day*, shuttered two months after its launch earlier in 2016, loomed large: 'It wasn't a very auspicious climate for launching a new newspaper.' With fear of monetary overcommitment in mind, the group launched the paper as a 'pop-up', initially to run for four weeks.

'We'll do it for four weeks and it'll bring us a lot of good publicity,' Kelly, who was the paper's launch editor, remembers saying. Their hopes weren't tremendously high: 'We might sell a few copies. It might break even.' The first issue hit shelves on Friday 8 July 2016, two weeks after the country had awoken to news of the vote to leave the EU. The timing is, Kelly claims, 'actually a world record for the launch of a new newspaper'. It went out, costing £2, and when the first edition's sales figures came in, the circulation director called to say they'd sold 40,000 copies, which was 'beyond our wildest expectations'. Kelly says, 'We knew we were on to something at that point.'

The figures didn't stay quite that high, but they remained distinctly healthy ('the break-even point was very low because it was part of a big organisation') and the paper graduated from pop-up to permanent fixture.

Kelly had, he says, a very clear idea of who the paper was for. It was right there in the tag line, which was, at the paper's inception, the newspaper 'for the 48%'. It was a 'niche product' for a 'niche market', says Kelly, but it had an audience. 'I had in mind the type of person who felt not just angry but furious – [but] actually more than that, felt hopeless at what had happened and felt a sense of despair and wanted to do something about it.' Kelly was clearly reasoning along similar lines to the academics Robinson, Watts and Moss: disappointed Remainers had a very substantial emotional investment. It made them a community. If you were looking to sell a newspaper, it made them a market.

'It may sound a bit corny,' Kelly admits,

> but I used to say that the journalism was great, but it wasn't the quality of the journalism that made [the *New European*] a success. It was the quality of the hope that it represented. It represented a kind of beacon that all was not lost and that every week you could get through your letterbox, or at the news agent, a concrete representation that you weren't alone.

That's what newspapers are for in general, Kelly thinks – 'they are small, little communities' – and for the 48 per cent, 'people who were feeling bitterly alone and dismayed at what had happened,' the paper was 'really valuable'.

The *New European* sold well, but there was room for other media formats in the Remain landscape, notably podcasts, which were by 2016 well on their way to the starring role in political commentary they now enjoy. The journalist Dorian Lynskey hadn't, however, particularly expected to be hosting one. He had been at Glastonbury when the Brexit result came through. The weather, he remembered, was bad, and when, late into the evening, he saw friends checking the news with 'faces like the weather', he knew the result was too.

'Everybody I knew was angry about Brexit,' says Lynskey, who at that point had spent his journalistic career writing primarily about music. In 2011, he'd written a history of protest songs. Early in 2017, however, he was approached by the founders of a new podcasting company, Podmasters. The men, Andrew Harrison and Matt Hall, wanted Lynskey to host a podcast about Brexit, alongside former *Economist* journalist Peter Collins and the commentator Ian Dunt, who was increasingly carving out a niche writing about Brexit (in October 2016, he'd published *Brexit: What the Hell Happens Now?*).

Lynskey hadn't met the others before – he says he 'hit it off' with Dunt at their first meeting, which took place at a Leon in Victoria – but the offer was appealing. The idea of the podcast as it was pitched to him was 'just to give people information, because [Harrison] felt that there were loads of people who were instinctively Remainy but didn't actually know that much about the EU, which was a big problem during the referendum'. In this, it echoed what Kelly termed the *New European*'s aim to give its readers 'ammo' for conversations about Brexit. The podcast would be 'quite funny and informal, but you'd have proper information' about Brexit and the EU. It would be called *Remainiacs*.

By, Lynskey says, 'complete coincidence', the podcast launched 'just as Theresa May declared the election'. The first episode was titled 'The empty tyrannical genius of Theresa May' and aired on 26 May 2017. The snap general election had been called on 18 April and by the time polls closed on 8 June, May had lost her majority. As Lynskey remembers, before the election most Remainer politicians 'were like, oh well, that's that. There was really no opportunity for a fightback. All these opportunities only opened up after the 2017 election, just a few weeks into the life of the podcast.'

Remainiacs was far from the only podcast focusing on Brexit. *The Guardian* had launched *Brexit means…* in December 2016 and the BBC began putting out *Brexitcast* in June 2017. But *Remainiacs* had a winning formula; it was buoyant and angry and encouraged listeners to 'own the remoan'. From the get-go, the podcast had a 'liveliness' to it, Lynskey says, and became, quite quickly, successful. 'I think it had quite a lot of listeners quite early because there was nothing else … that had that mix of analysis and sort of activism,' says Lynskey.

In October 2017, having put out just twenty-two episodes, the show announced it had hit half a million listens.[3] They also began doing live shows, touring the country and often appearing with special guests – at their 2019 'Democalpse' live shows, the guests were radio host James O'Brien and actor Mark Gatiss. The podcast had an 'explanatory purpose', Lynskey said, but also an 'emotional purpose, that it would give people somewhere to come and be cross about it, but hopefully laugh about it.' It was listed in *The Guardian*'s best politics podcasts of 2017, where it was described as a programme 'unashamedly for the 48%' and a 'wry celebration of the remoaner creed "for everyone who knows that leaving the European Union won't be *un morceau de gâteau*"'.[4]

They had conversations about whether to bring on a pro-Brexit contributor, but the view of the presenters and producers was, according to Lynskey, 'you get that every day on the radio. You get a back and forth. And we didn't want a back and forth. We basically want to be like we are Remainers, and we want to have a conversation among Remainers.' Brexit had been, in Lynskey's estimation, 'a body blow to liberal opinion' and the podcast helped people cope with that blow. 'The comment we had most of all from listeners was, you kept me sane.'

They didn't add a Brexiteer, but they did bring on other contributors. One early joiner was Naomi Smith, who had been an accountant for the first part of her career but in 2015 was so concerned about Europe that she 'just felt in my bones that I couldn't carry on doing what I was doing as a day job. I was so worried that we would have a Leave vote.' She went to work for an organisation called Business London, trying to wrangle businesses into publicly backing a Remain vote. 'It was very, very difficult,' she says, in part because 'organisations like the CBI felt very burned by being involved in the Scottish referendum a couple of years previously.' Smith described herself as having been a 'Charles Kennedy Liberal Democrat' at university but had been fairly anti-coalition and had moved away from party politics in the intervening years. She was approached by *Remainiacs*, who were looking for someone, as she describes it, 'who's quite funny and can joke about the awfulness of the situation, but who is also massively Europhilic in their worldview'.

She fit the bill and she remembers the experience fondly: 'I just loved having a safe space once a week where people who agreed with you could just turn to each other and go, this is mad. Like this, this whole endeavour is going to hurt a country. Can we just be honest about talking about that.' This is something she describes as having been 'hugely cathartic'. Smith also echoed Lynskey's scepticism of the need for balance on the show. 'The faux balance of the media' at the time was, she says, 'just completely irritating … you would have somebody who'd been a member of the European Commission or an expert in constitutional European law at a prestigious university being platformed alongside somebody who was, you know, a UKIP voter from somewhere who just hated the bendy banana issue'.

Another contributor who joined the team was Ros Taylor, who had been a *Guardian* journalist but was at the time of the referendum editing the LSE's Brexit blog. In that role, she says, she tried hard to strike a balance but admits that 'the idea that there was any possibility of being balanced on an academic blog about Brexit is for the birds. There were just so few academics who thought that it would be a good thing.' (Given that reality, she does think the blog managed to reflect 'the balance of opinion in academia'.) Her observations here seem to bear out the points made by Robert Saunders and Anand Menon about the failures of academia when it came to leaving the European Union. It was through this role that she found her way into the different, notably unbalanced, world of *Remainiacs*.

Taylor liked doing the podcast, finding it something of a contrast: 'It just felt very liberating to be among people who were saying, "This is a shit idea, and we're not afraid to say so," and I enjoyed that kind of energy in the room.' She adds, caveating that she feels she sounds 'horribly pompous', that she felt it was 'a moral duty to say, look, a hard Brexit is just self-inflicted pain and the UK voted for Leave without it ever being made clear that we'd have to quit the single market' whenever she was offered the opportunity to do so. To her, it felt 'like a social justice issue. Why the hell were politicians wasting time on this self-indulgence? … Brexit felt like a way for Britain to avoid talking about our real problems. I still get really angry about that.'

She clearly has, however, some reservations about the way *Remainiacs* talked about Brexit and is measured, even rueful, about the anti-Brexit movement. Their listeners, she says, were 'people horrified by this really stupid thing that we were doing and by the lies of the Leave campaign,' but the topic 'became such a marker of identity that it was impossible to get any common ground'. She describes feeling pleased at being able to be active on an issue she cared about but simultaneously being 'deeply frustrated by the identitarian turn that the movement took'.

Lynskey was also wary of being engulfed by the logic of the hardcore anti-Brexit movement. 'There were these, sort of, semi-celebrities who came through, whose whole thing was to talk about [Brexit] all the time, sometimes in the most hyperbolic terms,' he says. 'I think there was a bit of audience capture. It's like, well, that's what people want you to be, to be the very angry' anti-Brexit person. So, that was what they'd do. Lynskey, however, was clear that his job was 'to still be a journalist and to interview people and to, you know, moderate the panel discussions and so on'. In some ways, he said, he felt 'quite uneasy' about the podcast's campaigning angle. 'I'm not an activist here,' he remembers thinking, 'even though perhaps we are part of this sort of movement'.

The doubts of the *Remainiacs*, and their decision to keep the debate between Remainers, echoes some of Matt Kelly's sentiments over at the *New European*. 'If you take the *New European* as a publishing opportunity,' he says, 'then talking to yourself, talking to like-minded people, that is the business opportunity. You're never going to get Brexiteers to buy the *New European*.'

Kelly goes on: 'We once had [pro-Brexit businessman and political donor] Arron Banks write a couple of columns for us.' They reasoned that 'we should pay attention to what these people are saying'. However, Kelly remembers, 'The reaction we got from doing that was appalling. We lost loads of subscribers, [with] people writing and saying, you know, do not taint my *New European* with that scumbag.'

Kelly clearly isn't blind to some of the problems this insularity presents when talking about the pro-Remain demographic as the base of a political campaign. However, he doesn't view it as such a problem in a media outlet, fairly commenting that 'you would never get the *Daily Mail* editorial conference saying, well, maybe we should let them hear the other side of the argument. That would never happen, but it happens all the time in left-wing progressive media.'

Lynskey is very much aware that as one of the hosts of *Remainiacs*, he was the conduit, or possibly the enabler, of a mass of not always completely healthy public emotion. 'I think there are certain events,' says Lynskey, that people at the time 'don't realise the capacity of them to sort of drive the culture a bit mad.' The example he gives is the aftermath of Princess Diana's death in 1997 (and Tony Blair's corresponding enormous popularity), and says he thinks the Brexit years at their height had something of this as well. Similarly, Smith thinks the podcast's purpose was 'to provide a home for people who felt immense grief' about the vote and its consequences.

The podcast is still going – as of October 2020, it's titled *Oh God, What Now* – and is still clipping along quite nicely in terms of listens, with Lynskey and Taylor still involved. 'I'm sure there are some old-school *Remainiacs* listeners that maybe don't listen to us anymore, who think that we should have become, you know, Rejoiniacs,' says Lynskey. Luckily, there is a podcast for those people. There are two podcasts for them, in fact.

The *Remainiacs* and the *New European* were fairly substantial media hitters; they might have loosely focused on one topic, but their audience was not limited to people who owned bEUrets. They were talking to people who knew what they thought and wanted to hear their opinions discussed, but who were, on the whole, not living lives dominated by anti-Brexit activism. On the more homespun end of things, however, one finds a podcast which is now titled *Single Minded Rejoiners* but was, in the years when the debate over the second referendum raged, titled *Sixteen Million Rising*. Its host and producer is a man named Ben Chambers, who describes himself as having a background in 'teaching and music'. He is in his forties; affable and earnest, there is something of the Cornetto Trilogy about him.

As is common among people who became very involved in the anti-Brexit movement, he says he 'wasn't really politically activated or motivated in any way before the referendum. I voted in general elections, [but] I probably wouldn't bother with the locals.' He describes his political perspective as being generally 'left of centre, progressive'.

'I didn't understand all the pros and cons of either leaving or staying,' he says, but 'when you look around you and you see people like David Attenborough and Gary Lineker and pretty much every prominent, credible celebrity and politician advocating for remaining,' that made it seem, to him, like the obvious thing to do. He also felt that the referendum was tantamount to asking the electorate 'a really crazy question. It wasn't our job to get this one right or wrong, because we didn't have all the facts.' After the referendum, he became increasingly drawn in to the debates, listening to, among other anti-Brexit figures, the philosopher A. C. Grayling and spending time on social media connecting with others similarly concerned about the result of the vote.

After a time, he 'set up a little website, sort of collating all the evidence as to why this was a mistake, why we got this one wrong. I called it *Sixteen Million Rising* because, of course, there were sixteen million people, roughly, that voted to Remain.' In, he estimates, August or September of 2016, he did his first pilot show 'just gathering some of the voices of the people that were opposed to this'. Like the Facebook group 'The 48%' or the tagline of the *New European*, Chambers's focus on the 16 million who voted Remain bears out Daniel Cohen's point that insularity was a core feature of hardcore Remainers; they wanted to talk to each other and they created their own spaces to do so.

At the time of the referendum, Chambers was living in Bristol and became involved with Tom Brufatto's Bristol for Europe group and the growing Britain for Europe umbrella movement. The show was, and remains, very much connected with these local groups. It was, he explains, a place 'where people who, for example, were organising a street stall with Devon for Europe could send me a bit of audio and I'd stick it on'.

Subsequently, however, he moved home to Norfolk to help

his parents wind down their business and support them in retirement. Being at something of a loose end is, I have found, another common factor in heavy anti-Brexit campaigning. The movement was a place for people to give their time in a way that felt engaged and meaningful. Chambers, with some time on his hands, began to work more on his radio programme, often travelling to interview people. (Confusingly, despite being very much a podcast as we would understand it, it styles itself as a radio show. Chambers admits it's 'basically a podcast and it's not actually a radio show. I only call it that because I include licenced content'.) Britain actually leaving the European Union didn't have much of an impact on its output. In fact, whereas previously it had been going out every month, in 2020 he upped production and began to put out an episode a week (the episodes are two hours long).

As the years went on, he began to include more music, having realised 'that the number of bands and artists and singers and songwriters producing music about this was phenomenal'. In 2022 and 2023, Chambers was also involved in organising a pro-European online music festival called 'Music Sounds Better With EU', which also has a Christmas spin-off, 'Christmas Sounds Better With EU'. One of the artists he namechecks is the Marsh Family, a family singing group who went mildly viral in late 2024 due to a misjudged reworking of Paul Simon's 'Fifty Ways to Leave Your Lover', with lyrics changed to be about the Gisèle Pelicot trial.

Chambers says he tries to 'combine the light-hearted with the serious elements. There's always four or five tracks, four or five comedy clips. I would say I try and keep it light.' However, he notes that 'some people find it cheesy'. When he first started doing it, he says 'trolls' would pop up and say it was 'so Smashie and Nicey', a reference to the comedy characters played by Harry Enfield and Paul Whitehouse. (I have to confess, while I was not trolling Ben Chambers on social media in 2017, 'Smashie and Nicey' was exactly what popped into my head when I first listened to his programme.) He says he has a 'very small number of subscribers' but is dogged about promoting his show.

Chambers is an active participant in the Rejoin movement; the fight, to him, very much did not stop when Britain left the EU. He is involved in organising the National March for Rejoin, which was due to take place for a fourth year running in autumn 2025 but was rescheduled to June 2026. The reasoning here was ostensibly to hold off for a blow-out gathering on the tenth anniversary of the vote. Having attended successive marches and seen numbers decrease over time, my suspicion is that dwindling organisational capacity may also play a part here.

The march also has its own affiliated podcast, the second of the two hardcore Remainer podcasts discussed in this chapter. It is called *Rejoin Rants* and it aired its pilot episode at the end of 2023. Hosted by regular Rejoin March speakers Peter Corr and Lisa Burton, it's not as frequent as *Single Minded Rejoiners* – there are currently only nine episodes available – but guests have included Femi Oluwole, Mike Galsworthy, Steve Bray, Gareth Kearns, online anti-Tory personality Supertanskiii and Brendan Donnelly. Having decided to spend a year of my life thinking about the anti-Brexit movement, looking at the list of names was somewhere between seeing the names of all my cousins written down and scanning Oscar nominations in the newspaper: famous yet intimate.

PART II

THE GROUPS

CHAPTER 4

FOR OUR FUTURE'S SAKE AND OUR FUTURE OUR CHOICE

Femi Oluwole would become one of the second referendum campaign's most recognisable figures. Speaking at marches, doing media interviews and garnering, at the time of writing, almost 400,000 followers on X, formerly Twitter, for his breathless, outraged brand of pro-EU content – best described, I think, as attempts to turn Brexiteer populism back on itself, offset by a devastating, not unendearing earnestness – he is the only person profiled in this book whose 'Remain fame' was such that he came to be known mononymously. On social media and in the conversations of activists, he was, simply, Femi.

In 2016, Oluwole was a law and French graduate, working at Domino's over the summer after finishing an internship in Brussels the previous spring and waiting for another placement abroad to start in September. As soon as he knew there was going to be a referendum, he felt, he tells me, an 'emotional pull' to get involved and get campaigning. He started posting about the EU on social media; in the week before the referendum he had 'grown from maybe twenty followers on Twitter to about fifty,' but, he says, 'I knew that wasn't enough.' He decided to take to the streets: 'I went into the middle of Birmingham, Birmingham Bullring, bought a T-shirt from Primark and drew in felt-tip pen, "EU questions: Just ask."' His stunt, talking to members of the public about Brexit, would give Oluwole both his first taste of media attention (it made the *Irish Times*) and how he would spend much of the following few years.

After that, he 'climbed the pole of Twitter', posting 'commentary on stuff that people were saying but also just graphics that I made myself, screenshots of the relevant pieces of EU law'. He describes the philosopher A. C. Grayling as his biggest 'Twitter daddy', boosting his content and getting him an ever-larger audience. (My attempts to contact A. C. Grayling for this book were not successful. His mind is, one assumes, on higher matters.) Another way that Oluwole got on people's radars was 'calling up Nigel Farage on a regular basis and getting him to admit all lies that he told, inventing new names, new everything, to try and get through their screening processes. And that was fun, and it was effective. I was filming myself and recording.' He didn't, however, get through to Farage at a particularly impressive ratio. 'There were a total of five calls that I did over that twelve- to eighteen-month period… I must have called at least 600 times.'

Eventually, he created a second Twitter account, alongside his personal one. He called the new account 'Our Future, Our Choice' and through this came into contact with a man named

Felix Marquardt, who was, as Oluwole puts it, 'somebody who knew Andrew Adonis'.

Marquardt and Adonis put Oluwole in touch with Lara Spirit and Will Dry, two school friends who were now students (Spirit at Cambridge, Dry at Oxford) and who had been, with the quasi-patronage of Andrew Adonis, thinking about how they could campaign against Brexit. They were of the view that the deadlock in Parliament after the 2017 election created a moment of opportunity and that young people could make a useful intervention. Neither had very strong connections with political networks. Dry was a Conservative with a novel narrative as a regretful Leave voter, while Spirit hadn't been involved with any political parties or clubs at university beyond a term as social secretary of the Amnesty International society, having focused mostly on her degree and on playing tennis. Along with a fourth (and more short-lived) founder, Calum Millbank, Dry, Spirit and Oluwole formed Our Future Our Choice (OFOC), one of the two youth organisations affiliated to the People's Vote campaign. Oluwole was its official spokesperson.

Across the course of the post-Brexit period, Charlie Atkins worked for Open Britain, Adonis and the People's Vote campaign; he is now a SpAd in the Labour government. He described Adonis's role in the formation of OFOC as being key in 'putting people in the room'. The Labour peer had 'an infinite amount of energy,' Atkins remembers, and was 'putting these young people that had a cause but didn't really know which lever to pull, putting them in a room with people that could be like: if you can prove that you are a viable proposition, we'll give you a little bit of money or introduce you [to people who could help]'.

Felix Marquardt will not feature again in this book and I was, tragically, not able to reach him for interview (he is my white whale). He is, nonetheless, one of the most interesting side characters we will encounter. His involvement, as a French man in his forties, in founding a UK-based youth organisation, would remain relevant – particularly in regard to the way that organisation was seen. OFOC would forever be dogged by accusations that it was an 'astroturf' grouping, not an organic young people's anti-Brexit movement.[1] This was an aspersion famously cast on it by Aaron Bastani but also by several people interviewed for this book. When I spoke to James Schneider, who was Jeremy Corbyn's head of communications throughout this period (and who was and remains very critical of the second referendumers), he took this view on both OFOC and FFS, describing them as 'astroturf elite projects': 'They didn't represent young people in any way, shape or form, apart from in the fever dream imagination of [journalist] Toby Helm and the front page of *The Observer*.' If you are sympathetic to the case that it was an astroturf campaign, Marquardt (along with Adonis) is one of those doing the astroturfing. And so, a brief detour from OFOC for the Felix Marquardt story.

Marquardt was born in Paris in 1975, the scion of a wealthy family, and has had a varied career. He ran a rap label in the late 1990s called Kohiba; it was, however, not very successful and so he used the artists to help run a search engine optimisation company of the same name to help fund the label. According to a 2012 profile in French newspaper *Libération*, most of his SEO clients were porn websites; essentially, the rap artists just sat around googling 'tits', 'fuck' and similar.[2] The company was eventually shut down after being sued by the mayor of Paris for redirecting searches of the mayor's name to a pornographic website.[3] After stints at the *International Herald Tribune* (in a 2013 French television interview, he admits to lying on his CV to get the job) and L'Oreal (where, Marquardt has suggested, his ideas were not understood), he and his brother founded PR firm Marquardt & Marquardt, through which he set up a kind of Davos supper club called 'Atlantic Dinners'. In an interview about the dinners given to *Vanity Fair* in 2013, the author writes that at Davos, Marquardt 'seemed to be everywhere'.[4]

He converted to Islam in 2003 and, in response to the Paris attacks of 2015, founded a think tank aimed at reforming the religion. He referred to it as the 'Davos of Islam'; the organisation was condemned by ISIS, which led to Marquardt being given police protection.[5] In 2021 he published a book, *The New Nomads: How the Migration Revolution is Making the World a Better Place*, and he now runs Black Elephant, an 'experiential social network based on vulnerability', which basically seems to consist of going for walks and talking about your feelings. He has talked publicly about being in recovery from drug addiction, having 'used drugs every day for … twenty-five years'.[6]

Most relevant for us, however, are his involvements with youth engagement and European politics. In the early 2010s he formed *Barrez-vous!*, a movement designed to encourage young people to go abroad. With controversial former '68er turned MEP Daniel Cohn-Bendit, he founded an organisation called Europeans Now – in a 2013 op-ed, they argued that 'the time is ripe for a transnational, transgenerational, transpartisan, grassroots and crowd-funded movement to take European integration to the next level,' adding that 'before forming a party, we should look to Europe's success stories to determine what our platform might be' – and another organisation called Youthonomics.[7] Marquardt was Youthonomics's forty-year-old executive director; styling itself as a think tank, it issued a global ranking of countries by economic offering for young people (Norway and Switzerland came out top in 2015).[8] It was through this inevitably short-lived, youth-focused enterprise that Marquardt came to be involved with setting up OFOC. His involvement was fairly brief but long enough to leave quite a vivid impression on many in the space. 'Basically he wanted to run things in ways that we didn't. We didn't feel comfortable with his vision; it wasn't quite ours,' Oluwole remembers. After Marquardt's ejection, fittingly for an ex-Davos man, 'he went quite super villainy with the things he was saying'.

In 2018, Oluwole left his job in Vienna to return to the UK and campaign full-time. Lara Spirit didn't return to university after the Christmas break in 2017 and Will Dry similarly took time off from his PPE degree. Oluwole made a viral appearance on Sky News and the group's four co-founders were profiled in *The Guardian* in February 2018. Linked in the article is Oluwole's fundraiser to support his campaigning for a 'vote on the final deal'.[9] In forty-six days, it collected almost £13,000 in donations. The group were now locked in to campaigning for a new referendum on Brexit full-time. At first they worked out of Best for Britain's offices, but in April 2018 they would be brought under the umbrella of the People's Vote campaign.

Mike Galsworthy of Scientists for EU, who we will meet in Chapter 8, would be their office mate in the People's Vote campaign and offered me a thorough rundown of the OFOC crowd. To his view, it was

> such a shame that Calum [Millbank] left early because he was kind of like the coolest, the most chill, the most like natural, most street. I got on well with Will. He was very intelligent, sometimes would be a bit unpredictable on things but you could always talk to him. Lara was just lovely but a little standoffish and cagey often. She wanted to protect herself from that kind of environment, I think, and so didn't open her heart too much to most people, but she was always cool. I got on really well with Femi, but at the same time, I felt that he was often selfish at the time. I get it that it was a moment to seize, but it sometimes felt like others in OFOC were the helper elves for the Femi show.

When I asked one OFOC staffer about their day-to-day tasks in the run-up to the 2019 election, they explained, 'For me, it was scheduling campaign events with spokespeople that we had, like Femi, it was about sending Femi somewhere, arranging sending Femi somewhere, arranging some press to go and see Femi be somewhere and booking interviews for Femi,' which would seem to bear out this assessment.

Galsworthy thought:

> That's getting weird and I thought, Femi, you're far too self-interested instead of community-minded. I told him all this fairly recently, because he's chilled out a lot since then. He was really high intensity at the time. But I got on with all four of them; I liked all four of them.

Besides being locked in to fighting Brexit together, Oluwole and Dry were also locked in in another way: along with another OFOC staffer, they were living together in London. Oluwole, who was at the time turning twenty-eight while the others were in their early twenties, described the situation as somewhat 'stressful':

> We were all living under the same roof and working together, and you're living with all of your colleagues in a 24/7 campaign. So, there was literally no downtime. And this is all I will say – I had been through four years of uni and almost four years working abroad, living by myself, living with two people who had just left home, essentially.

Tensions in the Little Brother House aside, the group was, from April 2018, out of its odd beginnings and a part of the People's Vote campaign. Just as OFOC's staffers would have to get by under one roof, the organisation itself would have to work out how to share with another group that was both very similar and very different.

For our Future's Sake (FFS), meanwhile, came out of the National Union of Students (NUS), with its founders – former Falmouth Students' Union president Amanda Chetwynd-Cowieson, former NUS vice-president (VP) Richard Brooks and former Haringey Council cabinet member Jason Arthur – all being well acquainted with the labyrinthine ins and outs of the UK student movement. It's in their CVs, but it's also in the way they talk, as only a certain kind of seasoned student hack does: when I interviewed them, Brooks and Chetwynd-Cowieson both dropped the definite article that most people, including myself, would put in front of 'NUS'. They also stressed that they come from a particular part of the NUS. They aren't Labour Students or 'nolsies', a term deriving from the acronym for 'National Organisation of Labour Students', who, within the NUS, tend towards the right of the party; former NUS president Wes Streeting is probably the ur-nolsie. They aren't on the organised left either – where most of Another Europe is Possible, who we are shortly to meet, had spent time – but a secret, third thing: 'organised independents', generally Labour-sympathetic but not aligned.

When I interviewed him for this book, Brooks was a pollster; in the interceding period he has become a SpAd for the Attorney General, Lord Hermer. In early 2018, however, he was working for a youth engagement charity and often found himself in the pub, talking about Brexit with his friends. They were 'unhappy' that it was happening, full stop, but also unhappy with 'the state of the debate', which Brooks recalls as feeling 'very disparate from people's actual day-to-day lives ... we felt like, as younger people, the people who were talking about our futures weren't representative of us'. Chetwynd-Cowieson, who at this time was working for a student union in London but looking for a new challenge, strikes a similar note, saying, 'Every time you looked on the TV,' the 'people who were on whatever politics show' were 'always five fifty-year-old white men saying the same thing, the same arguments, arguing about issues that I know are important to some people, but never even bothering to touch on issues that are important or that really resonate more with, like, women under the age of thirty.'

Across a few pub trips, the idea of students and the student movement getting organised around Brexit metastasised and was taken up by, among others, NUS VP for higher education Amatey Doku, who was seeking re-election at the organisation's annual conference in March. He and those campaigning for him thought it was time for the EU to re-enter the student political scene.

His campaign manager was Luke Myer. In 2018, Myer – since July 2024 the Labour MP for Middlesborough South & East Cleveland – was a sabbatical officer at Edge Hill University. Living between university and where he's from (and where he now represents) in Teesside, he says he saw two very 'different worlds' when it came to perspectives on Brexit: one very pro, one very anti. 'I wasn't a massive Europhile,' he says, 'and in fact, I'm still not,' but says he 'really did believe as a democratic principle that it should go back to the people at the end'. Like everyone else who worked in the space, the 2017 election was what changed his perspective on the possibility of influencing Brexit. 'I think everyone up until that point where May lost her majority was sort of thinking, this is a done deal. But then, after that point, the truth is that anything could have happened.'

He recalls that he, Doku – whom Myer describes as having been keen on taking up the then extremely nascent People's Vote position – and others campaigning for him 'settled on [the EU] as a big thing that was affecting so many students across the country, this idea that they wouldn't be able to travel and study abroad,' as well as being aware of 'the impact of it on postgraduate students, on research collaborations and things'. In Myer's view, 'there was so much work that needed to happen to negotiate a better settlement for students and also just to try and give students a bit of a say' that just wasn't really happening. By February 2018, they'd hashed out a skeleton of Doku's priority campaign.

At the NUS conference in Glasgow, the campaign was launched – or, at least, the idea of a campaign was launched. 'It was a WhatsApp group and an email chain' at that point, Brooks recalls. 'It wasn't anything hugely serious.' They did, at least, have a name: they decided to call themselves For our Future's Sake, shortened to FFS. Brooks, who everyone I have spoken to credits with the coinage, remembers that they wanted something 'fun and punchy' and 'memeable'. He, I think accurately, describes the name as being 'very of its time, sort of like mid-to-late '10s' and reminiscent of 'Buzzfeed listicles' and a 'young millennial mindset'. Now, it seems a bit dated, but that's the problem with being very in touch with your own time; things will move on and everyone will become SpAds and your finger-on-the-pulse political youth organisation name will, merely six or seven years hence, sound as passé as someone replying with a GIF. But at the time, it struck a chord. Chetwynd-Cowieson remembers hearing it and thinking, 'That's so fucking perfect.'

One fairly distinguishing thing about the youth campaigns attached to the People's Vote campaign is that they never went through the period of soft-Brexit soul-searching and general positional uncertainty that many of the other organisations (most notably Open Britain) in the space did. 'None of us were particularly interested in customs union or single market arguments at the time,' remembers Brooks. In a statement that sums up a lot about the drive behind and problems of the campaign, he recalls, 'I personally found it boring trying to make the case for mitigating disaster to something that was only mildly bad.' He also felt there was simply not an appetite among the people they were aiming to mobilise – students and young people – for this 'very nuanced policy debate around the things around the edges'. These people thought it was terrible for them and their future prospects and they wanted their voices, saying that it was terrible, to be heard.

Brooks, Chetwynd-Cowieson and Arthur, with their loosely NUS-born campaign, were put in touch with Open Britain by Chuka Umunna just as it was readying itself to become the People's Vote campaign in spring of 2018. 'We essentially got asked to go and see Chuka Umunna,' Chetwynd-Cowieson remembers, and 'he was like, I hear you guys are starting up a campaign. And I remember being like, how?' James McGrory, director of the People's Vote campaign, was 'pretty won over', Chetwynd-Cowieson recalls, by their pitch and of the merits of having a grounded and experienced youth section of the campaign. They moved into Millbank Tower and got going. The deal was, Chetwynd-Cowieson remembers, that 'Open Britain would support with helping a couple of people work on it full-time, of which I was one of the first ones'. Soon after they began running their own crowdfunders, which, as with OFOC, enabled the hiring of more staff.

One of FFS's first big successes came in summer 2018, when they made the front page of *The Observer* with a story about how they had managed to get, Brooks remembers,

> students union leaders from something like eighty or ninety student unions to sign up for saying they wanted a final-say referendum. And then we briefed that into Toby [Helm] … it was our first real taste of, I guess, driving the news agenda, rather than just, like, having bitty stuff around the edges.

It was, Brooks says, 'the first front page of the People's Vote campaign' and was the thing 'that I was most proud of for the first, like, six months of the campaign'.

By April 2018, OFOC and FFS, who had had no prior

engagement with one another, were under the same roof and trying to do the same thing: mobilise young people to support a new referendum. They were both youth campaigns attached to the People's Vote campaign and working out of the same office, but despite, as one person involved put it, 'constant argument' over whether the two should merge, they were doing slightly different things to achieve their aim.

As Tom Baldwin recalls, 'OFOC were very good at stunts and getting media; FFS were really good at the organisational grind' (which, when grinding to aims such as signing up student union leaders to back a new vote, could also do quite well in the media). 'I think they had a lot more experience organising, especially with students,' one person involved with OFOC remembers, adding that FFS 'had more political experience than us as well'. To Tom Brufatto's view, 'OFOC's role often was to act as spokespeople that would go on TV at appropriate times,' whereas 'FFS had a network of student unions and the NUS who they worked with.' Chetwynd-Cowieson describes the groups as doing 'similar work but in a different way,' with OFOC 'a lot more focused on online content'.

The groups often collaborated on stunts, but despite collaboration and a clear division of labour, 'the two camps hated each other a lot of the time,' attests Baldwin.

Interestingly, most people I speak to describe this as in reasonably large part a class thing. 'OFOC were posher, Oxbridgey,' remembers Baldwin. 'I think we ribbed them about it standing for Oxford Fuckers Off Campus. FFS was more of a redbrick, state school, Labour students' vibe.' One former People's Vote staffer characterised Spirit and Dry as having 'that incredibly British public school niceness but also a hugely impressive confidence for people so young,' mirroring a comment made about Spirit in a 2019 profile in *Prospect Magazine*, which described her as having 'the kind of cultivated manners British parents pay tuition fees for'.[10]

'There was a real class thing,' remembers Brooks, who says it was

> hard not to draw comparisons between myself and other working-class people involved in FFS, the young black activists, [the] young disabled activist who we had in FFS and how they were treated, talked to, engaged with compared to quite well-put-together, posh, white Oxbridge graduates. There was certainly a bit of class awareness.

Luke Myer, who would end up as one of FFS's staff, strikes a similar note:

> I've got a lot of respect for those guys and there's some that I still work with today who've gone on to other things – but my perception at the time was that a lot of them were kind of middle class. They were very aware of the institutions of the EU but not necessarily the realities in communities like mine.

They wanted, Myer says, FFS to be 'deliberately quite different.

It was designed to be very diverse; it had working-class voices from places like mine, women, LGBT+ folks, people of all backgrounds as leaders within the campaign.'

Whether they played together nicely or not, a large part of the reason why the People's Vote campaign was happy to have not one but two youth campaigns was the movement's overall problem with attracting young people. As discussed, being anti-Brexit was, primarily, a middle-aged person's game. Young people were, as one Liverpool for Europe activist recounted to van Kessel and Fagan, 'noticeable by their absence'. A Leeds for Europe member noted that 'getting young people fired up about this is very, very difficult'.[11]

As a result of them being fairly thin on the ground, the campaign was 'super obsessed with young people', one former OFOC staffer remembers – at times to an almost parodic degree. The staffer remembers participating in a stunt when 'some German television [crew] came over and was like, "Oh, could we speak to you guys about, like, what you're doing?" So I said the lines that we said.' Afterwards, 'someone more senior from the campaign' came over and said, '"Next time TV films us, can you get one of the young people? And put them forward?"' The staffer remembered thinking, 'I'm fucking twenty-four!' Alas, twenty-four was clearly not young enough. The general view was, says the former staffer, 'we need young people, young fresh faces on there … get me, like, a kid'.

Some of those involved were genuinely very young. The barrister Jolyon Maugham remembers being struck by just how young Will Dry was – 'a kid' – when he spoke alongside him at an event. Some of them – 28-year-old Oluwole springs to mind – were, perhaps, only young when graded by the curve of the anti-Brexit movement. While it was a strength for the campaign to have young people involved, some people were concerned about using such young people to support the campaign in such a public way. 'I think we had a lot of responsibility,' one person involved in OFOC recalled, while 'being quite young'. Another senior staffer talked about having been 'worried' about putting young people in the media glare 'given that they've got to live the rest of their adult lives, whatever the outcome of the campaign'.

CHAPTER 5

INFACTS

In 2014, before that year's European Parliament elections, Hugo Dixon wrote a book called *The In/Out Question*. It was after David Cameron had given his Bloomberg speech, where he famously first called for a referendum on Europe, and the process of writing the book allowed Dixon to 'clarify his thoughts' on the forthcoming referendum. It's a Kindle book, available on Amazon ('I went through about six different editions,' the author says, 'as we went through different phases of the saga up to the referendum'). At present, the only endorsement is from Boris Johnson: 'Hugo Dixon is the Johnnie Cochran of the European Union – he has done a superb job of defending the indefensible!'[1] This would be a little baffling if you didn't know that Johnson and Dixon have been friends since childhood.

Having clarified his thoughts and reflected on the EU while writing his book, Dixon raised some money for the Britain Stronger In campaign and was, he says, 'a bit involved' in discussions in its 'early days', but he was discontented with the way the campaign was run. It didn't 'go for the jugular' and to his view, they 'weren't prepared to attack Boris and Gove'. He also thought Craig Oliver, Cameron's comms chief, had too much influence and divided motivations. Dixon reckoned that Cameron, with Oliver as his hand, 'thought he could kill two birds with one stone' and both 'win the referendum campaign' and 'keep the Conservative Party together'.

'I had no concern about keeping the Conservative Party together,' Dixon tells me, a statement – both with regard to caring about the Tories and caring about keeping parties in their current iterations – very much borne out by his CV. In the 1980s he was a Social Democrat Party (SDP) man. At the age of, he estimates, twenty-three, he 'was the chief policy adviser for Bob Maclennan when he was leader of the SDP, when it was tiny, when, basically, it split in two. David Owen decided he didn't want to merge with the liberals, and we decided that we did.' This Dixon had in common with his close friend Roland Rudd, who had also started his career with the SDP.

Following his youthful stint in the heady world of liberal politics, Dixon had spent most of his career as a financial journalist at *The Economist* and then the *Financial Times* (a bit of time at *The Economist* is a not uncommon thing in the world of the second referendum, I have learned). Eventually, he founded his own online news company, Breakingviews, and sold it to Reuters for '£12 million plus', according to reporting at the time (Dixon reportedly pocketed around £3 million from the deal).[2] By necessity, he says, while covering 'telecoms and financial services' in his journalistic career, the 'EU was always a dimension I considered'. To his view, Britain, which had been 'hugely influential in writing the rules' of the institution, would lose its influence and become 'rule takers' if it were to leave.

'It was not just an economic issue. It was also about power and influence in the world,' Dixon tells me. 'I remember the first referendum campaign, when I was a child and my mother was campaigning for it'. Dixon's mother is the artist Edwina Sandys – I interview him at his house, where a large piece of her art dominates one wall – Winston Churchill's granddaughter, which, as I'm sure readers can gather, makes Dixon the former Prime Minister's great-grandson. Edwina Sandys is also the daughter of Duncan Sandys, the Tory MP who we last encountered as the first chair of the European Movement. Duncan's daughter and Dixon's aunt, the former Tory MP Laura Sandys, was also a chair of the European Movement. This is all to say: Dixon is about as much an establishment pro-European as it is possible to be.

His mother, Dixon remembers, 'did an exhibition about keeping Britain in Europe, in whenever it was, '74, '75 or so', and says there has 'always been at the back of my mind a sort of general sense that we're going to be stronger if we are part of a bigger entity'. Concerned about Britain's EU membership and possessed of some doubts about the main Remain campaign, by summer of 2015 he had 'already started planning to create what was called InFacts'. 'We had a meeting here with [journalist] Will Hutton and various other people' to start putting it together. Dixon remembers Hutton saying, 'This campaign is going to be polluted by lies and by twisting of facts.'

'We never thought that this was the only thing that you needed' to win the referendum campaign, Dixon says, 'but we thought that as journalists, what we could do is we could try to set the record straight and try to get facts faster.' While obviously possessed of a political agenda, they tried to be fair-minded: 'We had a section called "…In Sins"', for when people 'on our side have actually got their facts wrong or twisted the facts'. This was not an irregular occurrence, as UK in a Changing Europe's Anand Menon explains: 'From the short-term Treasury forecast of April 2016 onwards, the Remain side had a tendency to exaggerate and to make things sound more drastic and more dramatic than they were ever going to be.' However, as Dixon admits, 'The fact was that 99 per cent of our fire was targeted on the Brexiteers and increasingly on Boris.'

They launched from (and initially worked from, although only for a few weeks) Dixon's house before moving into offices in Victoria Street in early 2016. (Dixon's residence, a beautiful mews house in west London, is not quite a character in its own right but will probably feature more in this story than any other private home.) Dixon put some money behind the venture, as did some of the other founding editors – a fairly august group, which included *Atlantic* journalist Anne Applebaum, former *Guardian* editor Alan Rusbridger and former *Economist* editor Bill Emmott. They hired some younger journalists, including Luke Lythgoe, former European Commission staffer Jack Schickler and Sam Ashworth-Hayes, now a *Telegraph* columnist. Rachel Franklin, who had previously been working in Brussels, served as Dixon's chief of staff. They 'had quite a good group of people,' Dixon reckoned.

The earliest article still accessible on InFacts's website dates from January 2016. Penned by Ashworth-Hayes, it is headlined 'MEP combats Brexit myths with UKIP fantasies'.[3] From then until the referendum, they turned out regular articles on the benefits of the EU and the problems with arguments put forward for leaving. Dixon, one of his staffers remembers, 'was always really keen on equipping politicians during the referendum with the right facts and stats,' mirroring Dixon's self-description elsewhere as a 'fact-based' Remainer.[4]

'He wanted a campaign that was fought on integrity and honesty,' the staffer told me, 'which is a noble goal – not often the best way to win a campaign, but it came from a very good place.' After the vote was lost, 'I think Hugo really wanted to do something positive,' they remember. 'I don't think he wanted to get sucked in to the … Brexit will do X to the economy' approach that had dominated much of the campaign and which many viewed as continuing in Open Britain.

In the immediate aftermath of the referendum, Dixon says he put InFacts 'into hibernation'. He then was involved in setting up an organisation called Common Ground. A 2017 interview with Dixon terms it 'a campaigning organisation designed to try to pull the country together again when other political forces are pulling it apart'. However, the article goes on to say, 'Common Ground, Dixon concedes, hasn't yet figured out how to do that other than visiting ten towns, which voted strongly for Brexit, to assess how they see themselves, strengths and weaknesses.'[5]

By the end of 2016, Dixon tells me, Common Ground had basically 'run out of steam', although it did subsequently produce a mini-manifesto. But Dixon continued to be involved in discussions about the future of the anti-Brexit campaign. When the 2017 general election created a new political equation for opponents of Brexit, this kicked up a gear. 'Before that election', Dixon remembers 'nobody had any hope'. He'd let InFacts 'tick along in the background' while he tried to complete an MPhil in philosophy that he'd interrupted to campaign in the referendum. I asked him what kind of philosophy he focused on. 'It's about the meaningfulness of life,' he said. Once the general election changed the state of play, they 'staffed back up again'.

I asked Dixon how he had come to be a supporter of a new referendum, an area on which he says his views changed:

> You couldn't call for a referendum immediately after losing one, but you could call for a referendum if it was a referendum on a deal that was being put to the British people. And we use various analogies, like, you know, you have a deal in principle to buy a house, but then you have the survey, you find that the roof is full of dry rot, you have the chance to pull out of the deal. So, we thought that the result of what the deal was should be the deal, or, in fact, if it was no deal, it should be put to the British people.

Having come to this perspective, he says, in early 2018, 'I was able to persuade Open Britain that what we needed to have was a new referendum.' Of this persuasion process he says, 'I persuaded Roland at Open Britain who's an old friend of mine and James McGrory, who was running it, and I think ultimately that I persuaded [Peter] Mandelson, who was also sitting on the board of Open Britain at that stage.'

After a few false starts and protracted discussions, InFacts came fully out of hibernation. When the People's Vote campaign launched in April 2018, Dixon's group would be one of its constituent organisations. Dixon, along with Franklin and a few other staff, moved into Millbank Tower with the rest. He also became vice-chair of the People's Vote campaign, under Rudd as chair. He would often write articles for *The Guardian* in this role, which would prove something of an issue within the campaign, as various people (notably Tom Baldwin) were unhappy with him having this title in the first place. When Baldwin was interviewed for UK in a Changing Europe's Brexit Witness Archive, he remembered

> Roland Rudd saying, 'Well I have appointed myself Chairman of the People's Vote Campaign' – in the same way that Idi Amin gave himself Victoria Crosses – or, 'My friend from college, Hugo Dixon, is now Deputy Chairman of the People's Vote campaign', which was news to a lot of us.[6]

InFacts sent out a daily email newsletter, through which the group would also fundraise, which covered similar ground to their website content, reporting on details of the Brexit process. They also kept active on social media – at the time of writing, they have 144,000 likes on Facebook and 17,000 Twitter followers. One person who was involved in writing the newsletter remembers the experience as 'tense', saying that the wider People's Vote campaign would often be unhappy with what they were putting out: 'Toning down the language was definitely one of the repeated requests.' They remember the tenor of these requests being to emphasise that 'we're not trying to stop Brexit. We're trying to give people a second vote, a second chance to vote on it.'

As this staffer's recollections indicate, while being part of the People's Vote campaign, in its day-to-day content and output InFacts was perhaps closer to the Remain media we discussed in Chapter 3 (albeit with a firmer link to the political asks of the Millbank organisation), very much serving the world of the already converted – and, indeed, incensed. Just how much utility they were actually providing, however, was to many people somewhat unclear.

One former InFacts staffer said they had joined the team assuming InFacts would be a 'fact-checking' and 'rebuttal' service within the People's Vote campaign, something akin to the fact-checking service FullFact but with an anti-Brexit focus. They say they soon realised that it was, as they put it, 'a talking shop personally dedicated to Hugo Dixon'.

Many I spoke to, including former InFacts employees, were sceptical of what the organisation actually did, as a constituent part of the People's Vote campaign. One former member of the InFacts team said that they

> got the impression that [Dixon] wanted to be an intellectual leader of some movement and he wanted people to gather around him to hear his views. But InFacts didn't seem to be fully part of the campaign, so no one was really sure what InFacts's end game was, other than to advance the interests of Hugo Dixon and boost his profile.

Throughout the period, Dixon wrote regularly in *The Guardian* and elsewhere, posting very frequent (at some points daily) articles on the InFacts site. 'I could never figure out what his related organisation was doing,' said one People's Vote staffer.

In this person's view, InFacts (while far from the only organisation in the space of whom this was true) was subject to what we would term audience capture and not entirely unhappy about it. 'If what you've succeeded in doing is monetising one particular segment of quite wealthy people's anger about something', they reckoned,

> then actually, when you're asked to use some of [those] resources to engage with people who sit outside of the monetised bubble that you're operating in, unless you're really committed to the campaign that it's in aid of, or you're good at thinking about how campaigns actually work, you're not necessarily particularly incentivised to share that resource.

In summary, much like other previously discussed Remainist media ventures, InFacts was on to a good thing talking to people who had no need of persuading.

Dixon had a close relationship with his old friend Rudd, but as chair of Open Britain's board, Rudd was not involved on a day-to-day basis. As such, Dixon was often seen as Rudd's man on the ground in Millbank. Not unrelatedly, the InFacts editor's relationship with the other denizens of the tower was not always smooth. It is safe to say that he was not, within the People's Vote campaign, universally beloved.

Richard Brooks noted that 'some of the content on the website was useful and it was good, and we used some of it' for FFS's briefings, 'but for the, I think the level of prestige, that Hugo probably wanted … I would suggest he wasn't adding as much value as he thought he was.' People's Vote staffer Bashir Ibrahim's view was that 'Hugo was someone who thought very highly of himself'. This was a phrase I heard more than once in relation to the InFacts founder; one former InFacts staffer described him to me as 'one of the strangest bosses I've ever had in my life'. The journalist Henry Mance reported that Alastair Campbell 'was heard to say, "If a computer designed someone to annoy me, you would get Hugo Dixon."'[7]

Tom Baldwin clearly has no love for Dixon and mentions that his office in Millbank was filled with 'all this naked art painted by his mother,' which he describes as 'quite weird'. Tim Shipman reports a female staffer as saying, 'There were definitely bare breasts in one of them … Women for a People's Vote would have to come in and sit under these boobs.'[8] As one former staffer bluntly puts it, people on the campaign 'fucking hated Hugo Dixon. They used to relentlessly make fun of him' and thought he was 'a spanner'. (In the staffer's own, more moderated, opinion, Dixon 'seemed a little bit odd'.)

InFacts wasn't a one-man band – as discussed, it had various staff and affiliated journalists – but it was certainly Hugo Dixon's show. It was not, however, his only show. From around the middle of 2018, Dixon began to host regular dinners at his house. He would invite a 'mixture' of people but recalls that 'we had journalists as much as possible', both from the UK and from Europe, because he wanted to 'persuade people on the other side of the Channel that it wasn't a lost cause'. They always had the same thing: salmon en croute and a green bean and pea dish.

One person from the campaign who attended the dinners described them as an attempt to do 'salon-form politics, which is, I think, quite unique and a bit of a relic.' They describe the format: after arriving at Dixon's 'very beautiful house', the guests would 'all sit around and Hugo would kind of chair the conversation, and there'd be various journalists there from lots of different publications'. Per one attendee's memory, it was 'lots of quite posh people saying really random stuff while eating salmon en croute'. They thought 'it was bizarre, but it was free dinner, so I went'.

Conversation, however, was not always to the line of the People's Vote campaign or, in the view of some who attended, even particularly grounded in the realities of the situation. Baldwin 'came once, I remember, and just visibly was … completely overwhelmed and bemused,' says one person who attended. He spoke, but the attendee remembers his intervention as 'so striking, because it was just Tom obviously being implicitly like, that's not our message'. He then 'I'm pretty sure, walked out early'. They speculated, I think correctly, that Baldwin was 'quite irritated by it'.

CHAPTER 6

SODEM

For many in Britain who were following the Brexit debates in Parliament, one man came to represent all the chaos, absurdity and strange inescapability of the period. This man is not really an influencer of the kind we met in Chapter 2 because he does not trade in online content: he is a creature of the physical realm, most specifically the 100 metres or so around Parliament. His name is Steve Bray; it's possible you're more familiar with him as the Stop Brexit Man, because that's what he spent years of his life yelling at Parliament, the media and anyone passing by. Almost a decade on ('We're into our eighth year of protesting,' he said on a podcast in spring 2024), his voice is undimmed, though often aided by a megaphone, and you can still find him holding forth outside Parliament, wearing a battered top hat.

He uses speakers, blasting out parody versions of popular songs with lyrics about Brexit, which have latterly seen him fall foul of new laws about protest and noise pollution – laws which some people suspect might have been written with him in mind. Given just how much racket he has kicked up within the hearing of the MPs who run Britain (not to mention their staff), I consider this not unlikely. He is now a fixture of Westminster life.

In the Brexit years he was there every day; more recently, he limits his appearances to sitting Wednesdays, when he and his protest group, SODEM, take over a small traffic island just outside 1 Parliament Street, festooning it in flags and banners. SODEM stands for Stand of Defiance European Movement, but you are meant to pronounce it like 'Sod 'em'. They are very easy to spot, holding large signs, some of which are standard anti-Brexit fare (lots of references to the elephant in the room and shooting oneself in the foot) and some that are so specifically topical as to be meaningless to the outside observer, even the fairly politically clued-in one. On one visit to their traffic island, I found myself trying to parse the meaning behind a large print-out image of the Labour MP Chris Curtis, who had appeared on *Newsnight* the evening before. It was something about Brexit, probably. SODEM wear bEUrets, of course, but I have also seen starry bucket hats, wristbands, and faded blue and yellow shoelaces. Everything at their encampment, including the people themselves, has a much-worn, exposed-to-the-elements look to it. They come by this honestly: that's how you look when you've been standing there for years, and they have. Their anti-Brexit T-shirts have that muted, bobbly, endlessly rewashed look.

Bray was, at the time of the Brexit vote, living in Port Talbot (he was born in Cardiff) and working as a rare coin dealer, having previously been an air force brat and then spent the first part of his working life as an engineer. Despite repeated efforts, I wasn't able to interview him for this book. While easy to find – standing outside Parliament, wearing a top hat and yelling – he is, as he told me one afternoon while eating a sausage roll and holding a placard, generally pretty busy, and getting an hour with him proved too difficult. However, he spoke at length to *The Guardian* in 2022 and appeared on the *Rejoin Rants* podcast, discussed in Chapter 3, in 2024.

He was, for most of his life, not particularly politically engaged: he had never been to a protest before and told the hosts of *Rejoin Rants* that he 'was never political until the referendum' and indeed that 'when they announced the referendum, I actually at that point didn't know which way I'd go'.[1] It took Bray, he remembers, 'a few minutes of looking online. [In] less than twenty minutes, I was full-on Remainer.'

Having done his research online, Bray knew how much funding the EU had put into Port Talbot, as he told *The Guardian* in 2022. Where he lived was 'one of the most deprived areas of the United Kingdom, and I was shocked at people there: that the majority voted to leave'.[2] Initially, he aired his anger about the vote and what it might do to Port Talbot on the internet, mostly arguing on Facebook – but, he told *The Guardian*, after a time he decided 'to move offline because I wasn't achieving anything. It was just arguments and trolls. It took up so much time and it achieved very little.'

In the real world, Bray became increasingly active. He began to attend protests and, as *The Guardian* reported, 'volunteered to drive a float from a carnival in Germany – featuring a huge model of Theresa May with a gun in her mouth – around London and Norwich'. He pitched up outside Parliament after the 2017 election, having done a stunt that involved spending no money and sleeping in Hyde Park for a week to protest May's confidence-and-supply deal with the Democratic Unionist Party.

SODEM has no formal structure – it's very much the house that Steve built, or perhaps the lean-to that Steve built – but if there is a number two in the organisation, it is a man named Gareth Kearns. He and Bray appeared together on the *Rejoin Rants* podcast in March 2024; describing their relationship, Kearns said, 'I just go where he tells me.' If you have passed by SODEM's encampment, you may recognise Kearns; he has long silver hair and is often wearing a blue and yellow keffiyeh. A former actor from Milford Haven, he has a voice for projecting. Overall, he cuts a distinctive figure, looking a little like Lucius Malfoy and sounding like Steven Toast. He often climbs up onto the railings at the top of the traffic island and stands and waves a flag, like a man standing at the prow of a ship. He is the captain of his ship, the master of his fate. (He isn't. That's Steve.)

Kearns tells me that prior to his involvement with SODEM, 'the only time I'd sort of gotten off my bum and shouted about something was against ID cards'. He says that his unhappiness with Brexit stemmed not even so much from the thing itself but 'the way it was done, the rank dishonesty'. To Kearns's view, 'If anyone is going to be that dishonest about how to go about something, God knows what the hell they're hiding.'

He'd seen the protesters on the television while following Brexit and said he'd found there to be 'a great deal of charm about the idea of these people who just go up and do it'. Kearns first 'turned up outside Westminster' during December 2018, when Theresa May's indicative votes were before Parliament. 'I had met various people there,' Kearns tells me, 'and I did say, I'll come back in January. So I came back in January. And there was a group around Steve.' There were 'six of them all together', who were the 'core group'. Another thing that brought together Kearns and Bray was a keen class awareness: both take pride in their working-class backgrounds. Kearns talked to *Rejoin Rants* about how he felt when anti-Brexit campaigners are branded members (and servants) of the liberal elite:

> I've had that thrown in my face so many times, and sometimes I have to say to people, I was a secondary modern schoolboy. I went to the same secondary modern school that my father attended. You have been drawn into this by public school boys. How the hell am I the elite?

Over the course of spring 2019, Kearns 'made himself very useful to [SODEM] in lots of different ways'. They were, he says, 'long days', often protesting news broadcasts happening live around Parliament. 'Studios on stilts' were constructed to cover events and 'Steve [was] coming up behind things, with big things on poles, sticking them behind the camera. And, of course, we're shouting, and we're getting long, long poles and sticking the flags behind the people as they're doing their interviews.' Bray told *The Guardian* he was there to get the message out: 'If you can't be seen, you've got to be heard. In shutting me out, they are actually making it a bit worse for themselves.'

Anand Menon of UK in a Changing Europe was often one of the commentators having his appearances disrupted. 'There was the whole issue of trying to broadcast when what's his face was there with his megaphone,' he says. 'You know, there were moments when it got quite unpleasant out there – people were quite abusive.'

Menon also remembers thinking to himself, as he passed the SODEM perma-protests on the way to do his broadcasts, 'Don't these people have jobs?' Many were retired – Kearns, who is in his fifties, admits to being 'one of the youngest members' of SODEM, explaining that the group contained 'a lot of people in their sixties, seventies and, in the case of one, eighties'. But plenty, including Kearns, juggled a fairly intensive schedule of protesting and working. Across the spring of 2019, Kearns fit his protesting responsibilities at Westminster around his work. In that period, he remembers, 'I would get up, I would go to the protest early, help out with the protesting, the sort of breakfast television period' and then head to his job in a different part of London but be back in the evening. 'Me and a couple of people were … often there for *Newsnight*. You're getting to 10 and 11 o'clock, there would often still be people with lights'.

Interestingly, because they were so present and, in their own way, quite extreme, the SODEM crowd often came into contact with extreme protesters of a different persuasion. When I interview him towards the end of 2024, Kearns asks me if I have ever heard of a man named Peter Lynch. When I say no, he explains that Lynch recently died in prison, having been sentenced for rioting following the Southport stabbings. 'We encountered him various times,' says Kearns, including on the day that the UK left the EU, when 'a bunch of his mates sort of, set on me, mugged me' before being stopped by a policeman. Lynch was 'a very nasty piece of work,' Kearns thought. He told me that he had been at a 'Tommy Robinson rally' and seen that 'Peter Lynch has been deified. They've got a great big presentation up on the screens about it. He is their first great martyr.'

Louise Brown of North East for Europe would also travel down to participate in SODEM's protests, fitting this around her job as a speech therapist. While Brown notes that the tactics of SODEM are very different to those of the European Movement, she felt that lots of different approaches are needed and can compliment each other. 'The visuals of SODEM have been used over and over again in the papers,' Brown says. 'The archive footage is used all the time. They still use the pictures.' She jokes that 'we would be very rich' if they were paid royalties. Speaking to the SODEM regulars, this media visibility – they keep an eye on which outlets use their images, on how much reach they are getting and can tell you which Google image searches will bring up a SODEM placard – is clearly important to them and is as much of a theory of change and impact as you will find in Bray's set.

I spent quite a bit of time at SODEM's camp while working on this book, hanging out with and talking to the rag-tag, rotating dozen-or-so activists who show up every Wednesday. One afternoon, towards the end of my time writing this book, I arrived to find they'd been exiled from their normal traffic island by road works and were over on the pavement across the road, near the phone booth that was in one of the *Harry Potter* films and therefore attracts a perma-line of tourists.

They were playing music at deafening volume – they're due back in court soon, I'm told, as part of ongoing disputes over the noise levels at their protests. An older man in a T-shirt reading 'Rejoiner' danced vaguely, holding an EU flag on a long pole. Bray tells me they've moved more into satire of late. He was on the mic, playing the likes of Funboy Three's 'The Lunatics (Have Taken Over the Asylum)', the Kinks's 'Apeman' (it has a line about nuclear war, Bray explains, and we're closer to midnight than ever, so it's relevant) and Talking Heads's 'Road to Nowhere' (because Brexit has put the UK on the road to nowhere). Bray acts like a kind of DJ, providing commentary. His voiceover is often a bit fragmented and odd. He is prone to trailing off and repeating himself, like some kind of anti-Brexit performance poet. 'Brexit,' he says at one point, before pausing for a long time. 'What a disaster,' he eventually concludes.

Sometimes DJ Steve plays the hits. When they put on 'Ode to Joy', the EU anthem, Kearns – who today has tied up his hair with a yellow scrunchie – and the dancing man sing along. They are really giving it something. Kearns has a good singing voice, and continues his performance when 'Brexit Tragedy', their reworking of the Beatles's 'Yellow Submarine', comes on. I think he is singing along loudly over a track that is in fact his own voice recorded over a version of the song with no lyrics.

While at the protests, I find myself often involved in conversations that aren't really conversations, just sets of people talking past each other on a preferred topic. It's odd, but you get used to it. On this day, for reasons I can't quite figure out, the topic is space. Donald Trump and Elon Musk want to colonise space. I'm told about this by three different people and nod vaguely. They are bad, Trump and Musk. I agree. It's bad that they want to colonise space. Trump would never have won without Brexit, I'm told. I nod.

I speak to one older man who tells me he has only been coming to the protests for a month (some of the people there have logged seven or eight years). In the '70s and '80s, when Britain was in Europe, the country was better, the man tells me. Things were easier: the food was better (now there is too much junk food, coming from America) and you could get a job much more easily. All you needed was your P45, and you could start looking for a job in the morning and have one in the afternoon. I believed it when Kearns told me he was their youngest member; even by the standards of the anti-Brexit movement, the SODEM set are old. But they are persistent.

The former Labour MP Lloyd Russell-Moyle thought Bray was 'great, absolutely marvellous, not because I really cared for his activities, but I think that it is a totally great British tradition that you have nutters participating in politics. One thing I loved, and other people hated about the Brexit debates,' says the former Brighton Kemptown MP, was that 'you stepped outside of Parliament and there [were] people wielding Liberty bells. They would ring them every minute. These were pro-Brexiteers ringing for our liberty. And then there was Steve Bray with his megaphone – that to me is the essence of democracy.'

Along with their protests in Westminster, the SODEM crowd also travels to the conferences of the different political parties. 'We make a special effort for the party conferences,' says Kearns. 'I can absolutely promise you that certainly about 80 per cent of the Labour Party is with us. And I think... 99 per cent of the Lib Dem party.'

Many of the groups surveyed in this book had meaningful connection with politicians and the media. This is not so for SODEM: they were not getting their press releases picked up, their messages taken into the parliamentary mainstream. Through sheer, bloody-minded presence, however, Bray and his gang inserted themselves into popular understanding of British pro-Europeanism. They were endlessly photographed, always loomed just in shot during broadcast rounds and soundtracked party conferences with their booming 'trolling songs'. Corbyn's former comms chief James Schneider remembers a 'horrible moment' when attending Labour Party conference in Liverpool a few years ago: 'I was in my hotel room, and I heard *O partigiano... bella ciao, bella ciao...* and I think, fantastic! The comrades have arrived! Something good is going to happen! So, I go downstairs to try to see what's going on. And unfortunately, it's Steve Bray.'

Captured in action on the pages of countless newspapers, the Stop Brexit Man became a key touchstone for how people in Westminster and beyond visualised the chaos of the Brexit years. As such, whether the denizens of Millbank Tower liked it or not – generally, they didn't like it at all – the broader project of resisting Brexit became, in the minds of many, bound up with the actions (and images) of Bray, Kearns and the rest.

CHAPTER 7

SCIENTISTS FOR EU

Two of the organisations that would make up the People's Vote campaign, Scientists for EU and NHS Against Brexit, were run by one man. That man's name is Mike Galsworthy. Given his large social media following (he easily fits among the ranks of the influencers and micro-celebrities discussed in Chapter 3) and the fact that he is now also chair of the European Movement, it's safe to say that Galsworthy is, in the anti-Brexit space, something of a big cheese.

It wasn't always so. Galsworthy's early career was not in politics. 'I did my university degree in science – natural sciences at Cambridge,' he tells me, 'and then I went on to do a PhD in behavioural genetics at KCL.' He then spent several years working abroad in Slovenia and in Switzerland, moving slowly from research into EU science policy in the process. In 2013 he came back to the UK and became involved with Scientists for Labour in the run-up to the 2015 general election. He 'ended up being on the executive and then writing the policy for Scientists for Labour' at that election.

After the defeat, he says, he took a 'don't mourn, organise' approach. 'I said, look, we can't do anything for Labour for a good few years, but there is going to be a referendum. We should move fast. We should set up a new campaign, do it on social media, call it Scientists for EU and then basically get scientists involved.' There was, he remembers, one other person, a man named Rob Davidson – who, his HuffPost bio says, got a 'PhD at the Institute of Cancer Research in London and who has worked at the University of Birmingham' – who said, '"That sounds like a really good idea" – so Rob and I founded Scientists for EU together and drove it.'

By November of 2015, Galsworthy says, he managed to get funding for the group from 'David Sainsbury, because he loves science and is pro-EU'. As Galsworthy remembers,

> my main pitch to him was, look at Leave.EU and what they're saying. They're doing terrifyingly well on social media, particularly Facebook. Look at their engagement. Look at the placeholder campaign that Stronger In has put up. It's not competing. You need more on our side and there needs to be organic communities.

Galsworthy was of the (for the interviewees in this book, anyway) unusual opinion that having the vote was a good thing: 'Unlike most of my peers, who raged, "Why did Cameron ever do that?" Because if you believe in democracy, the citizens should be involved in absolutely everything, and if you think it's too complex, then maybe we should have spent more time explaining EU mechanisms.' This is something which, he says, 'governments never did and the BBC never did. All that education went begging, even during the referendum; it was just a four-month dash.' It was, he felt,

> absolutely fair to have the question, but the way that the political parties had dealt with it and the way the BBC had dealt with it, it wasn't structured conversations community by community, the science community, the fishing community, the tech community, the farming community, right? It was far too often a BBC gladiatorial battle between old white men from the Conservative Party that were for Remain and for Leave.

Before the vote itself, Galsworthy and Davidson put together 'two business plans' for Scientists for EU: 'One for if we win, one for if we lose. If we'd won, then there would have been a UK presidency of the EU in 2017 and we could lead a whole open data drive.' If they lost, Galsworthy said, 'I thought the immediate thing I need to do is be responsible to the community, to get testimonials of damage being done, because there would be, and get that out to the media and also weave plans for how much UK–EU science relationship can be salvaged.'

As we've discussed, most people in this book spent a time after the referendum operating on the assumption that all they could do was hope to soften the worst excesses of Brexit. This was not Galsworthy's view:

> I didn't need to do all the kind of kneel before Zod, 'I respect

> the referendum result' penance that politicians were being made to say but which a huge number of people, who felt the referendum was based on lies, resented. I could be completely distant on that, because I would always say, right, what I need to do now is help the science community and so that's what I focused on right after the result.

This approach is one of the many things that marks out Galsworthy as a creature of the grassroots, an allegiance and way of thinking that would shape his path throughout his time involved in the second referendum and anti-Brexit movements. He says he was 'an accepter' of Brexit without feeling the need to say '"I respect the result" … I accepted it and even though I didn't respect the content of the contest, I respect democracy and had to adapt.'

Galsworthy and Davidson were also behind an organisation that was initially called Healthier in the EU, but which after the vote became NHS Against Brexit. 'I had an interesting battle with the Department of Health' over it, Galsworthy remembers. 'They tried to get me to change the name and eventually couldn't.' The problem was, he explains, that the NHS said his organisation was using 'the NHS brand and logo, and I proved that I wasn't and showed other campaigns that were using the NHS name that they hadn't gone after. And I offered all these, kind of like, minor changes and sent them back lots of questions until they gave up.' There had been some reporting in the right-wing press on this 'interesting battle', and Galsworthy ultimately prevailing was, he says, 'not what the *Express* [newspaper] expected, because they'd already been crowing that, you know, we were nobbled'.

Despite Davidson's presence (although he would not stick around for the full duration of the campaign), there was generally the impression that Scientists for EU and NHS Against Brexit belonged to Galsworthy. As one person involved in the campaign described it to me, the Scientists for EU group was 'literally just Mike. That was him. He had a Twitter account and he somehow created an organisation.' Galsworthy was online in all formats; several people commented on the YouTube videos Galsworthy would post of himself reading out poetry ('It's got an odd energy,' one staffer told me contemplatively). Some were pejorative about more than just his poetry; one person I spoke to described Galsworthy as 'something of a zealot', adding that

> there's this wonderful warming sense of being experts and being right that people wallow in a little bit. And I just found that slightly unpleasant to be honest … We are scientists. We know what we're talking about. The clear implication being, you're not scientists. You have no idea what you're talking about. I just found that the tone could verge on the slightly patronising.

Galsworthy was hugely active on social media, across Facebook and Twitter. When he talks about Scientists for EU's role within the People's Vote campaign, he describes it in explicitly social-media related terms, as the 'page with by far the most engagement on Facebook. So, we really were the social media engine – and relentlessly promoted other pro-EU groups.' As one People's Vote staffer put it to me, Galsworthy, like Oluwole, 'had that real ability to ride the social media wave and provide content that a sizeable minority wanted to watch and were energised by, so gotta give him his dues for that'.

In 2019, Galsworthy explained to me, 'I raised about £400,000, mainly from David Sainsbury but also from some other high-net-worth individuals, to invest directly in the build-up of local groups, specifically on their Facebook pages.' To Galsworthy, for all that people derided online efforts, this was where the action and the organising were happening.

Owing to his passion for social media, and alongside his roles at Scientists for EU and NHS Against Brexit, Galsworthy was and remains a big exponent of #FBPE, the hashtag that came to symbolise for many the less strategic and more cringe excesses of the anti-Brexit movement.

FBPE was the brainchild (brainpost?) of a man named Hendrik Klaassens. On 25 October 2017, Klaassens posted, '#ProEU tweeps organise Follow Back Saturdays! Type #FollowBackProEU or #FBPE if you want to get more #ProEU followers. Let's do this!' Picked up by a series of pro-Remain accounts, it quickly spread and soon became a recognisable calling card of hardcore pro-European sentiments online. As Galsworthy remembers, someone sent him an early iteration of the hashtag and said:

> 'Hey, Mike, you should be getting on this.' And I thought, ooh, hold on a sec. If everyone who's pro-European is following back each other and strengthening each other, then we aren't reliant on elitist figureheads that we have to all support to get anything heard. We're actually cohesive and we [are] strengthening each other's voices.

Galsworthy describes the hashtag as

> a beautiful way of knitting together a big army online that can move together, see what each other are doing and empower each other to have bigger followerships and have their own voices ... finding new people in it. So, I did a lot of videos promoting that. And it really ... took off, to the point whereby it thoroughly irritated a whole load of Brexiteers that suddenly there was this big cohesive ... voice that was just everywhere on Twitter. That was very, very effective, as well as working with local groups and making everything cohesive.

Galsworthy was so enthusiastic about it that he even wrote an article explaining the merits of the hashtag for the *New Statesman* in February of 2018. '#FBPE will help spread awareness fast in the Twittersphere,' he wrote, concluding that 'Britain has a new cultural community rising. It's pro-EU. And #FBPE is part of the glue.'[1] In the article, Galsworthy described Klaassens as 'a Dutch member of the pan-European group "Progressive Europe", which wanted to combat right-wing populism on social media'. Interestingly, #FBPE is not the only bit of hardcore anti-Brexit culture exported from the Netherlands; the boy band The Breunion Boys (singles include 'Britain Come Back'), which formed in 2018, are also a Dutch product.

The writer Séamas O'Reilly penned a piece about the hashtag for *The Fence* magazine in 2020. He described it as 'a convenient vehicle for signal boosting their collective message, useful in a British media environment incapable of skewering the lies, false promises and outright incompetence of Leave and the UK government'. O'Reilly went on to term the hashtag 'a megaphone chain of users, on hand to amplify facts unmentioned in the starkly Leave-leaning printed press, or stories inadequately covered in the more sober, balance-obsessed broadcast media'. However, he also noted that 'those four letters also held within them the original sin of the #FBPE brand; a sense that, in asking for follows, there was within its central premise something shot with desperation'.[2]

While Galsworthy is not wrong that the hashtag provided a locus for online Remainers and boosted their followerships – I was struck, reaching out to activists I wanted to interview for this book, how many of them had notably large follower counts on Twitter – I think O'Reilly is on the money in his assessment that its central premise was 'shot with desperation', a kind of unstrategic grabbing at support, animated by a mindset that views any expression of pro-EU sentiment – a post, a parody song – as a win for the cause. The voice that it summoned up may have been effective for yelling at Brexiteers, but it was also alienating to pretty much anyone who wasn't a signed-up member of the hive. It was this, along with the sense that it was a vehicle primarily used by people who were not very good at speaking on the internet, who couldn't quite get the tone right in a language they'd only recently taken up, that made #FBPE a by-word for the excesses and downright weirdness of out-of-touch Remainers. The hashtag was in many ways the drive to insularity discussed in Part I – media and influencers and a grassroots base who wished to speak only among themselves – made internet flesh.

The debatably useful #FBPE was not the only hashtag Galsworthy promoted. 'I helped a bunch of people set up … the pro-Corbyn, pro-EU hashtag PCPEU. I said, "Look, you don't need to be in with FBPE. You can be pro-Corbyn and pro-EU on your own terms. Make your own gang to make your own arguments."' This was against the backdrop, Sarah Jones remembers, of 'the FBPE crowd goad[ing] each other on demonising Corbyn'. As she remembers, the animosity was so great that they 'wouldn't stop even when we won and [Corbyn] agreed to give us a confirmatory referendum with Remain on the ballot'. Richard Brooks remembers a similar dynamic: the FBPE set were, he says, 'actively anti, and quite vocally anti, Corbyn's leadership,' which 'wasn't helpful'.

Because of how early – pre-referendum, as discussed – Galsworthy's groups were on the scene, and because of the funding they had from Sainsbury and others, the former research scientist with a flair for social media was on the ground floor of discussions about where the anti-Brexit movement should go. In 2017, trying to set a course of action, the great and the good of this world would meet, Galsworthy says, around a copper-topped table at the headquarters of the Resolution Foundation.

I asked Galsworthy when it was that he became persuaded the right thing to do was to campaign for a new referendum. He says he did an interview with Owen Jones in early 2018, where he

> said the public should retain the right to pull the plug on anything the government does if they don't like what the government is doing. I really dug into what the emerging 'final say' strand of thinking meant. And lots of people around the table at the Resolution Foundation saw that and said, that was great. And Peter Mandelson wanted a meeting with me after that – he'd say, you know, how do you think we should do this? So, I think, for him, that that lit up a bulb.

You will notice that Hugo Dixon, speaking in Chapter 5, is of the view that he and not Galsworthy persuaded Mandelson of the need to push for a second vote. I leave readers to make up their own minds on who was moving the dials.

As such, whoever's idea it was, when the umbrella organisation was formed, Galsworthy's groups were a part of it. Owing to his connections and standing in the grassroots, he worked with Tom Brufatto 'doing the big sales job to all of the local groups about why this makes sense, why this is a good idea'. Speaking about this task, he echoed the sentiments of Brufatto (with whom, over the Millbank period, he would increasingly find himself allied): 'A lot of the grassroots local groups were extremely wary' about coming in and working with the other organisations, particularly Open Britain.

But, as we've seen elsewhere, coming in to the People's Vote campaign didn't mean instant harmony and mutual respect. Many people expressed doubts about the utility of Galsworthy's groups when it came to mobilising for a second referendum. One Millbank staffer I spoke to said of NHS Against Brexit:

> If I was running NHS Against Brexit, one of the most diverse employers in the world, and it's the biggest employer in Europe, the audience that you have got there to mobilise, or even just understand and talk to and work with … it was one of the biggest topics of the [referendum] campaign and then never quite actually became one of the defining topics of the negotiation, which is bizarre. And like, if I had access to that brand and to build that mailing list and all the things you need for a successful campaign, that could have been really powerful for the People's Vote as a whole.

They went on: 'I could not tell you what they were doing. I honestly couldn't tell you what they were doing. Mike Galsworthy was just on Twitter, and then, because he got a big following and our media is quite basic, managed to get himself [in the media] quite a lot.'

Mike Galsworthy was perfectly aware that not everyone could see the point of what he was doing: 'Tom Baldwin got the sense that the grassroots respected me and I liked the grassroots. But that was it. I mean, I don't think he actually understood or knew what I was for or why I was hanging around. He seemed to think of me as a bit of a spare wheel.' Despite, as we will discuss further in Part III, often finding himself seriously at odds with other parts of the People's Vote campaign, Galsworthy remembers the period fondly.

'Even though they were really stressful and messy years,' he says, there was lots he 'really loved' about it. One such thing was how, 'unlike during the referendum, after the referendum there was this explosion of new characters, and I thought that was great fun, and that's why I like the grassroots and the activists, because you saw these characters come out, you know, there was life to it, there was soul to it, there were new people coming on the scene'.

CHAPTER 8

BEST FOR BRITAIN

Best for Britain began to be formed shortly after the referendum result in 2016 but wouldn't publicly emerge into the world until 2017. It differs from the other organisations in this section, in that it wanted not to represent a minority strand within the pro-European movement – young people, scientists – nor to provide a distinct service within it – Remainer agitprop, constant protest on Whitehall – but to act as a hub in its own right. Eloise Todd was its founding CEO and was also involved more generally in getting the project off the ground.

After an early career stint working for the Social Democrat group in the European Parliament, by 2016 Todd was working at the One Campaign, the international development charity, in Brussels. After the Brexit vote she found herself involved in conversations about a new organisation; eventually, it was decided that she would run it, with former UN Deputy Secretary-General and member of the House of Lords Mark Malloch Brown as its chair.

'What I think should have happened during the referendum campaign,' Todd says, was the provision of 'a very clear space to understand what the realities would be' and to talk about 'what different forms of the relationship' with Europe might look like. It was that discursive space that Best for Britain wanted to build after the vote.

'You need to not tell people but show and bring them along,' says Todd of Best for Britain's approach. 'There needs to be a much more, almost like deliberate, not really campaign, actually, but a conversation, a conversation about Brexit.' This hearts-and-minds approach was one of a few things that would distinguish Best for Britain from many other organisations in the anti-Brexit space. Another was money. The campaign had very healthy public fundraising, as did almost all anti-Brexit groups, but by June 2018 the BBC reported that it had received £800,000 from billionaire George Soros and had overall '£2.4 million in its coffers.'[1]

In February of 2018, *The Guardian* speculated, 'Soros's decision to fund the group, rather than the higher-profile Open Britain, appears to be down to a personal connection with Todd through the international development sector.'[2] The chair of the group, Malloch Brown, was also, according to his IPPR profile, a 'close friend' of Soros and from 2009 served on the board of his Open Society Foundations.[3] Various people I interviewed noted how much money Best for Britain seemed to have. The group also gave patronage of various kinds to other groups in the space, including Another Europe (who received funding) and Our Future Our Choice (who in early

2018 worked out of their offices). As Luke Cooper of Another Europe is Possible put it, his organisation was 'one step removed from that world, but there were lots of wealthy individuals who were very committed to staying in the European Union and were prepared to put funding on the table' – among them Best for Britain's backers.

As a (for this book) rare organisation in place at the time of the 2017 general election, Best for Britain mobilised heavily around the vote, throwing themselves hard into running a tactical voting campaign. 'Sometimes there's moments in time,' Eloise Todd remembers thinking when the election was unexpectedly called, when 'you just have to act'.

Gina Miller, who was already known as an anti-Brexit campaigner following her successful Article 50 lawsuit that swiftly followed the referendum in 2016, fronted the campaign. 'We want to build the biggest tactical voting effort in UK history,' she told *The Guardian* at the time.[4] A crowdfunder to support this work was launched. 'We raised £400,000 from the public within a week,' Todd tells me (the BBC reported in 2018 that Best for Britain spent £353,118 between June 2016 and June 2017).[5] They were trying, Miller said at the time, to 'bypass the hierarchy of parties' and to just support candidates on the merits of their position on Europe. 'We are not party political,' Todd stressed in *The Guardian* in the run-up to the election. 'We stand for democracy in this country and a constitution that respects proper balance of powers and doesn't railroad the country into an extreme Brexit.'[6] This quote is telling, I think, of the pre-2017 election consensus among the anti-Brexit political class: there's no mention of a new vote or of stopping Brexit, only a mention of avoiding an 'extreme' exit from Europe.

The result was, of course, favourable for the anti-Brexit team. Theresa May lost her majority, there was a hung Parliament and a parliamentary majority for leaving the EU was now far harder for the Prime Minister to reach than it had been. However, Todd says that while she had expected that everyone was 'going to be elated because the Tory majority has been reduced, and we've now actually got a fighting chance of winning a vote in Parliament on a Brexit-related issue,' in reality 'a lot of the Remain, former Remain campaign, centre-left establishment, including some people associated with my own campaign and backers, everyone went really quiet'. The next move was theirs to make; they just weren't sure what it should be.

There was significant overlap in the work and aims of Best for Britain and Open Britain and, reputedly, a merger was proposed and discussed in late 2016 and early 2017. Clearly, they had the same aims in mind; however, differing approaches and clashing personalities kept them apart. I would speculate that the fact that both organisations had a distinct asset – Best for Britain its money, Open Britain the data left over from the referendum campaign, which will be discussed more thoroughly along with the organisation itself in a later chapter – that they could hold onto for themselves played a part in keeping them separate. Maybe they would have been stronger together, but given each possessed its own valuable core, they didn't need one another. The two organisations had, Amanda Chetwynd-Cowieson remembers, a 'love–hate relationship'.

A similar situation unfolded when it was time to form the People's Vote campaign – or not, as the case may be, given that the organisation Todd headed decided not to join up with the campaign. To Tom Baldwin's view, the People's Vote campaign 'should have included Best for Britain'. Todd was, he thought, 'suspicious of the People's Vote campaign. I think for quite good reasons, in that she thought it was a sort of Labour-right thing, possibly a precursor to a new party.' As a result of all this, Baldwin says, 'there was a bit of antipathy between the two organisations, but we got closer over time'.

In Baldwin's view, Todd 'rightly spotted that people like Dixon and Rudd were wankers'. Todd made no comment on either when I interviewed her but said she had a good relationship with Baldwin. Gina Miller, who fronted Best for Britain's 2017 election efforts, was not in favour of the People's Vote campaign ('I told them at the first meeting I went to that it was a terrible idea'), which did not improve relations between the two campaigns.[7] 'I am on record saying after the referendum, "Well, we're all Brexiteers now because you have got to respect the result,"' Miller has said. 'There was definitely friendly fire' from other pro-European groups, one Best for Britain staffer told me.

Todd, however, was fairly phlegmatic about the decision not to come into the Millbank operation. Drawing on her background in the charity sector, she commented that 'just because Oxfam exists doesn't mean Save the Children shuts down'. To her view, 'multiple campaigns is fine'. 'Do I believe that we failed [to stop Brexit] because we had two campaigns, not one? Not at all,' she says.

Despite not formally joining up, Best for Britain's thinking followed that in the sector more broadly: by 2018 they were, of course, supportive and actively campaigning for a new referendum. They would frequently collaborate with the People's Vote campaign on stunts and marches.

In late 2017, Naomi Smith, who we last met putting the world to rights with the *Remainiacs* in Chapter 3, was asked to join the organisation. As she remembers, 'Best for Britain approached me to say we need a COO and you're an accountant who cares about Europe. Will you interview for that role?' As she then understood it, the mission was to 'stop Brexit by any democratic means. Those means might be an election where the party that wins has a mandate to stop Brexit or do a very, very soft "stay in the single market" version of Brexit, or it might be a second referendum.' As time went on, this last option increasingly eclipsed the others in the anti-Brexit space and Best for Britain moved with the times.

However, even as the campaign became supportive of the new vote, it was with the hearts-and-minds approach that was always more present in Best for Britain's thinking than in the more organisational, goal-oriented world of the People's Vote campaign. 'The thing that always bothered me,' says Todd, was 'if we had got another referendum, would we be able to get people out in the numbers to vote?' Smith struck a similar note: they wanted to stop Britain leaving by any democratic means, rather than automatically going

> full throttle on another referendum. Having campaigned on the first referendum, I didn't think anyone had done anywhere near enough work to bring the country with us to secure a victory in another one. I was also deeply worried that bouncing straight from one into another without having done that groundwork could be dangerous.

There was also a cultural difference. Flo Hutchings began working as an intern at Best for Britain in 2017 while a master's student; once they'd finished their degree, they went back to the organisation and would eventually rise to be its political director after the 2019 election. As well as chiming in with Todd's view of the People's Vote campaign – 'I think we felt that there was a short termism in their approach or a narrow mindedness' – they remember the bigger umbrella campaign as being a bit of a 'macho space. And I think one of the things that stood out and that I liked about Best for Britain was that it always had a strong woman at the helm, and that was something that was kind of missing from the rest of the anti-Brexit space.' Hutchings mentions Baldwin and Alastair Campbell as they describe there being a lot of 'macho energy' in the sector. Naomi Smith recalls how, when she went to cross-organisational meetings, 'various men, and it was always men' would be 'saying we must have a coffee, I need to talk to you separately from all of this. And would then brief against their colleagues to me and then the other one would brief against the first one – and it just felt like an absolute vipers' nest.'

After the 2017 election, Hutchings remembers, Best for Britain's work at first focused mostly on 'trying to galvanise the pro-Corbyn and the Corbyn core of the [Labour] party to take a more anti-Brexit, less Eurosceptic approach'. When they came back to the organisation in 2018, 'we were doing more of the meaningful votes and trying to coalesce the Tory wets'. They had, Hutchings remembers, 'a big email list … I mean, I think [the] People's Vote one was bigger,' but Best for Britain's was 'pretty substantial, like, high hundreds of thousands'. They used this list to raise money and to rally supporters to contact their MPs.

Informed by their slightly more holistic, changing-minds approach, the organisation also worked to get stories about the harms of Brexit into the press. 'We didn't want to do top-down. We wanted doctors, nurses, teachers, local people in their local papers,' Todd tells me, saying, 'You know what? This might be a bad idea, because we're not going to have as many nurses in the hospitals.' Hutchings remembers that working in the press team 'was about gathering stories about what the cost of a no-deal Brexit was, or FOIing NHS trusts to find out how many nurses have left the trust since 2016 and doing those kind of data-driven stories about the impact of Brexit'.

Best for Britain also did a great deal of polling – usually, Hutchings remembers, 'broken down by constituency … what constituents' views were on Brexit, what Labour voters' views were on Brexit. And then we'd use that data to go to individual MPs and say, you know, actually in Bishop Auckland, 95 per cent, 75 per cent, whatever, of your voters actually want a close relationship or want stronger economic ties' with Europe. As Smith recalls:

> Most of our energy was put into persuading Labour and [the office of the Leader of the Opposition], really. And so there was an enormous amount of work done there … keeping our tally of which MPs were overtly [pro a new vote], which were under the radar quite supportive but hadn't wanted to put their head over the parapet.

They were, she says, 'pretty much the only campaign' in that era conducting MRP polls of Leave/Remain intention. With those, Smith says, 'we were able to demonstrate to MPs, look how much things are changing in your seats'.

James Schneider, of Corbyn's office, took a dim view of Best for Britain's polling efforts, saying that they had spent a large amount of money on 'push polling, which misinforms the public, because the polling that went in their way, they gave to the so-called newspaper *The Observer* or other outlets, and the ones that didn't go in their favour, they just buried and never published'.

Todd had a background in the Labour Party – she had been a friend of the MP Jo Cox and was one of the founding board members of the Jo Cox Foundation – and this positioning was helpful to the campaign. Best for Britain, remembers Schneider, 'seemed to be, I would say, into the kind of softer bits of the Corbyn machinery' and 'were probably much better at getting in' to influence the party than the People's Vote campaign. He cites widespread antipathy on the party's left to Alastair Campbell as an example of the kind of problem Best for Britain didn't have to contend with, adding that Campbell was 'really the last person in the world who would be convincing wavering Corbyn staffers'. John McDonnell, in his interview for UK in a Changing Europe's Brexit Witness Archive, addresses these meetings:

> Anything I could do to prevent a major split, that is what I was doing, basically, even to the point of having regular conversations with Alastair Campbell. Hush my mouth! Lightening [*sic*] will strike. I even did an interview for him for his magazine and I am still getting slagged off on social media for that, but there you are. Things had to be done to keep everything together.[8]

The openDemocracy founder Anthony Barnett had similar feelings to Schneider on Campbell's involvement, writing in his 2017 book *The Lure of Greatness: England's Brexit and America's Trump* of an occasion where he saw the former spinner speaking at a pro-Europe march and reckoned that 'fluent in the cause he may be, but when he opens his mouth the souls of Iraqi innocents roll from his tongue'.[9]

By comparison with the ill-thought-of Campbell, Schneider says Eloise Todd – whom he assesses, basically correctly

I think, as being of the soft left of the Labour Party – could more convincingly make the case. She could say, 'I want social democracy; we have shared values. I really think that if you do this, honestly, it would be better for all of us in these ways, blah, blah, blah.' That was, Schneider says, always 'going to be a more compelling pitch'.

In May 2019, Todd left Best for Britain, having decided to run to be an MEP. She was second on Labour's European Parliament list in Yorkshire and the Humber, where she is from, after the incumbent MEP Richard Corbett. She describes the contest, with a kind of wry hindsight, as a 'lemming run'. You know things are 'out of whack', she told me, 'when you think that being an MEP will restore your work–life balance'. Todd was replaced by Naomi Smith, COO at Best for Britain, who remembers:

> Eloise wanted to run for the Labour Party in the Yorkshire and Humber region as number two on the list. And I don't think Labour had ever not got two MEPs in that region before. So I think the staff and board were all incredibly supportive of her doing that and assumed she would get in, and very sadly, she didn't. The board had asked me to be acting CEO while she was fighting the election and then when she didn't come back, they asked me to stay on as CEO.

In Labour's historic May 2019 drubbing, both Todd and the incumbent Corbett, in the number-one slot ahead of her, lost.

The organisation's noted financial heft was on show again

in the run-up to the 2019 election, where it spent significant amounts on Facebook advertising – £34,228 in one week alone in November 2019, the BBC found, for an overall spend of £659,475 between October 2018 and November 2019.[10]

At Best for Britain, Smith is still in place as CEO. Hutchings left in 2023, having spent, all in, more than five years at the organisation. As Smith remembers, after Britain did finally leave the European Union in 2020,

> the board took a very considered view on whether to wrap up and admit that we failed or whether to carry on. But by then, prior to that, People's Vote had obviously collapsed completely … and because we'd sort of stayed outside of that tent, we were in a much more robust position and the board felt that we had a duty to carry on.

While small, it is the sector's great survivor. Beyond vindicating the decision not to join the People's Vote campaign, I am not sure there is any particular lesson to draw from this beyond: have deep pockets and control yourself.

PART III

LABOUR

CHAPTER 9

THE CAMPAIGN INSIDE THE LABOUR PARTY

From the moment the 2017 election changed the parliamentary maths on Brexit, it was clear that the position of the Labour Party, with 262 seats to the Conservative's 317, would be key in any attempts to stop or soften Brexit. Left-winger Jeremy Corbyn had led the party since 2015, and the consensus was that he was at best not particularly animated by the issue and at worst actively Eurosceptic. He was also – following a disastrously unsuccessful leadership challenge by Pontypridd MP Owen Smith in the summer of 2016 that led to a firm reiteration of Corbyn's mandate to lead the party – at the height of his internal control. As Corbyn adviser Andrew Murray has written, at that point 'the Labour Party was at Corbyn's feet'.[1]

While it's wrong to say that the issue divided particularly neatly on factional lines, it is fair to say that historically, the left of the Labour Party has had a more live current of Euroscepticism than the party's right. Tony Benn, the grand old man of the Labour left and a key figure of influence on Corbyn, had voted to leave the European Community (EEC) in the 1975 referendum, as had the man who would find himself occupying the office of Leader of the Opposition in 2016. Corbyn, as a councillor in Haringey, had even put down a council motion opposing EEC membership back at the time of the first referendum.[2] Figures of the Labour right, both contemporary and historic but particularly those associated with Blair and Blairism, have generally favoured greater integration. Giles Radice, a fairly grand old man of the Labour right, even published a book titled *A Love Affair With Europe* in 2019 in response to Brexit, outlining the politics and emotional connection that had animated his lifetime of ardent pro-Europeanism.

In the 2017–19 parliament, there was a range of internal groups of different factional stripes campaigning hard for Labour to adopt support for a new referendum into its platform. Generally, they were regarded as either wreckers or dupes by a leadership which clung 'hubristically', the journalist Owen Jones has argued, to the idea that Brexit might damage Labour but would always ultimately be a 'greater existential threat to the Tories'.[3] When it came to Brexit, the Labour leadership didn't want to stake dramatic positions: as Labour's then head of policy Andrew Fisher has said, after the 2017 election, 'We weren't trying to make it an issue or the dividing line between us and the Tories.'[4] Oliver Eagleton's *The Starmer Project* gives a similar account. It argues that the leadership

> defaulted to mimicking the government's Brexit plan in an attempt to neutralise the issue. If they ensured there was minimal space between the Labour and Tory approaches, then Corbyn's

> strategists believed they could avoid falling into the fatal trap: a Brexit-dominated election that would split Labour's base.[5]

Many also read an ideological, as well as pragmatic, leaning into this positioning, viewing it as a manifestation of that Labour left Euroscepticism.

However, whatever the motivations, the leadership was swimming against the tide of party opinion. On a Venn diagram, the demographics of people who are members of the Labour Party and those of people who are exercised about Europe are basically a circle. They are older and they are middle class and they are liberal and often not that politically clued-in; the idea that Corbyn brought in a youth wave is also on shaky ground given the average age of people joining the party in the first year of his leadership was fifty-one.[6]

Poll after poll showed that Labour members wanted opposition to Brexit and backed a new vote. In July 2017 – almost a year off the formation of the People's Vote campaign and before any significant campaigning activity on the issue – 49 per cent of members 'definitely' wanted a vote on the final Brexit deal, while 29.4 per cent said they were 'more yes than no' on the idea and only 8.8 per cent definitively opposed it.[7] In January 2018, 87 per cent of members backed staying in the customs union and 78 per cent backed a second referendum on any Brexit deal.[8] The figures stayed constant: it was clear what the members wanted and it was not the constructive ambiguity favoured by the leadership. 'The horns of the dilemma we were on, was massive support amongst rank-and-file Labour Party members, both in terms of Remain but also then in terms of a second referendum, and then, back in our constituencies, that not being reflected amongst our constituents,' described then shadow Chancellor John McDonnell (who, it's worth noting, unlike Corbyn, Starmer and many other senior Labour figures, represented a seat that had voted to leave).[9]

Because it was unrepresentative, because it was perhaps not where they were politically and because many of the most pro-EU voices hated them, openly or otherwise, the top of the party would have preferred to ignore this mammoth support among the membership. A different leadership may have been able to do this better. Corbyn, however, had come in as an insurgent, the tribute and champion of member democracy, and believed, probably more sincerely than any of his predecessors, in a democratised party.

Those who wanted the party to take a more avowedly anti-Brexit stance sought to use this belief and activate members on the issue. I think there is some room for debate on how successful this was and how much of the reasoning behind Labour's ultimate position change in summer 2019 was down to dire results in the European elections. But, certainly, it troubled Corbyn to be on the wrong side of members, and particularly members in his constituency, and the pro-second referendum campaigners' aims were ultimately achieved.

The process, however, would be extremely arduous and riven with ill-feeling and factional suspicion. This chapter will walk through a variety of players in the internal Labour space, probably the most important of which began life several years previously, back before Corbyn was leader and before Britain had voted to leave the EU. Its formation was convivial: 'Me and Amelia had, I think, a glass of wine, maybe at the British Library, on a summer's day, and she was terribly late for the meeting, which wasn't a problem,' remembers Luke Cooper.

Cooper and Amelia Womack were meeting at the British Library to discuss founding what he describes as a new 'left current'. It was the summer of 2015. Cooper was a law academic and a veteran of the British left, who had, in 2012, won £60,000 in a libel case over false claims that he orchestrated violence at the 2010 student protests.[10] Womack was, as of the year before, the deputy leader of the Green Party, with a similarly long history on the left. David Cameron's recently won majority meant that a referendum on EU membership was grinding into view on the horizon, but despite this, 'to our surprise', Cooper remembers, there was no 'organisation that was arguing for Remain from an explicitly left perspective' yet on the scene. They wanted to set one up; their current would eventually grow into the campaign group Another Europe is Possible.

Michael Chessum was abroad in the summer of 2015, in 'Athens reporting on the [bailout] referendum in Greece, which was an interesting moment for an anti-Brexit left-winger to be there'. He knew that 'intellectually, very early on, I was quite committed to opposing Brexit'. He had posted something about it on social media and was invited by Cooper, who he knew from the student movement, to join an email chain, which became, Chessum remembers, the first 'steering group for Another Europe is Possible'.

'In the first twelve months or so,' Cooper says, 'we were a bit more Greenish in some ways'. The group 'got quite a lot of support from Caroline Lucas's office when we started,' due to Womack's involvement and connections. The campaign group Global Justice Now also became a supporter. 'At some point in the referendum campaign,' says Cooper, 'we got a decent link to John McDonnell and met quite a few different Labour MPs,' and the group 'became more of a coalition'.

After discussions via email and in person in 2015, the group had its formal founding conference in February 2016. Cooper recalls that 'Laura Kuenssberg turned up at our launch event and it made it onto the BBC News that evening,' with a 'thirty-second video of what's happening' (he speculates that 'they were just sort of covering any referendum event' at the time).

In the view of those involved with Another Europe (a view shared by the vast majority of people interviewed in this book), the designated 'In' campaign, Britain Stronger in Europe, was not good. It was, Chessum thought, 'shockingly bad' and also 'indescribably shit'. They had, he recalls, 'every single kind of hated, pro-austerity politician you could name' making the case for Europe; in his view, 'they may as well have put Darth Vader on the leaflets'.

In this context – a Remain movement all too happy, to the view of Womack, Chessum, Cooper et al., with a political consensus that was fine with austerity and hostile to migrants

– Another Europe is Possible felt it had a specific and important path to forge as a committedly left-wing but pro-European organisation. 'Much though it later took flak for being too much a part of that world,' Chessum says, it 'was set up specifically as an alternative to that, in an attempt to bring together Momentum, an attempt to bring together the Greens'. As one person involved with Another Europe interviewed by Fagan and van Kessel says, 'In terms of our background, our instincts and our personnel, we were the activist left doing Remain campaigning, rather than being a Remain campaign that was left wing.'[11]

Chessum, having come up through the student movement and been among the founders of the National Campaign Against Fees and Cuts (NCAFC), was in the 2015–16 period we're discussing also heavily involved in the newly formed Momentum, set up to support Jeremy Corbyn's leadership and generally push the left within Labour. He explains:

> I got involved in Momentum in Haringey, where I lived, and after a lot of wrangling there, ended up being elected to the regional committee. From the regional committee I got elected to the national committee, and in February 2016 was elected to the steering committee, and then eventually, on the steering committee was elected to be the national treasurer.

After the referendum was lost, Cooper remembers the organisation 'took the view that we would argue initially for a soft Brexit – like freedom of movement, single market membership and so on,' but like all organisations discussed in this book flipped to being out-and-out supporters of a new vote in the aftermath of the 2017 election. They got some money from the Joseph Rowntree Foundation in 2016 and 2017 and would also come to get money from Best for Britain. It was enough for, Cooper said, 'several staff', with Chessum serving as their national coordinator. They built an infrastructure and eventually set themselves up as a membership organisation, which brought in more funding. At their height in 2018, they had five staff in the London office and regional organisers around the country.

The Love Socialism Hate Brexit group was set up by MPs working in tandem with Another Europe, with Clive Lewis and Rachael Maskell from the 2015 intake and 2017 intake members Alex Sobel and Lloyd Russell-Moyle. Sobel was among the founders of soft-left grouping Open Labour, while the other three MPs were members of the left-wing Socialist Campaign Group. 'We created Love Socialism to help try and rally people,' Russell-Moyle remembers, 'that could be associated with the left or soft left, and to say this is a real pressure' over the Brexit issue that was not coming from the right of the party.

Their message was – unsurprisingly, given the grouping was in essence an extension of Another Europe, basically identical to that of the group set up by Womack and Cooper. As Clive Lewis wrote in 2019, 'Overwhelmingly, Labour members and CLPs [Constituency Labour Parties] agree with us – the Labour grassroots do indeed love socialism and hate Brexit.'[12]

As discussed, they knew their anti-Brexit message was popular with the membership and wanted to create the space to be supportive of the leadership while still being anti-Brexit. 'There was a narrative that was growing a little bit,' Russell-Moyle remembers, from certain sections of the left 'that at the time we thought had quite a lot of influence over Labour Party policy – I'm not sure we were necessarily right – but the feeling was that there was a narrative that if you're a true socialist, you were a secret Brexiteer.' What Russell-Moyle is referring to was commonly named 'Lexit', meaning left exit, a phrase coined by Owen Jones in 2015. This narrative ran down from the left currents who opposed joining the then EEC in the first place, through Benn and Corbyn, and was particularly present in some of the trade unions that backed the Labour leader. The now-general secretary of the RMT, Eddie Dempsey, accused Chessum of having 'pockets full of Soros money' in reference to Another Europe having funding that ultimately came from the Open Society Foundations.[13]

To Russell-Moyle's view, Corbyn was not going to be convinced by the 'intellectual argument' on Brexit. 'All the liberal commentators in the world, all they did was dig Jeremy's feet deeper into the ground.' What Corbyn and those around him 'respected was a show of force by people, by movements'.

'What mattered to him,' says Russell-Moyle, was 'social movements' such as protests, grassroots organising, motions through CLPs and member democracy. With this in mind, Love Socialism and its allies thought they could 'change the dial' by playing Corbyn's game on Brexit. 'There were some successes on that,' he says, but to his view they ran into trouble because the group expanded to include 'too many people who the leadership [saw as being] on the right' of the party.

The leadership in the wake of the Smith leadership challenge, Russell-Moyle says, had a 'bunker mentality' whereby 'everyone could turn out to be your enemy, your friends could become your enemy, but it was very hard to become your friend'. As he puts it, 'If you added one drop of bad blood into Love Socialism, that made you all bad blood, not the other way around. You didn't dilute the bad; you were just all infected by it.' This was a problem that dogged Another Europe throughout its existence: this sense, this suspicion, that it was laundering a right-wing attack on Corbyn's positions, and on the left as a whole, through the language of socialism, movementism and member democracy.

To the view of Schneider, Corbyn's head of comms, Another Europe was 'always a front organisation'. It was originally, he says, a 'Green Party front organisation, then it was a Global Justice Now front organisation, then it became a Momentum front organisation. Then it became a front organisation for the ruling class in order to destroy Corbynism. Objectively.'

'The idea in Michael Chessum's head was not "I want to bring down Corbynism"', says Schneider.

> Of course not. His idea was, 'I want to support Corbynism and I would like to see some social democratic reforms in my lifetime.' That would be nice. But nevertheless, the objective role he played and the objective role Another Europe is Possible

> played [was] more damaging than that of [Blairite group] Progress, because they gave left cover for obvious establishment Blairite politics to gain more purchase over wide layers of the membership, in a way which was never designed to benefit, never could benefit the party as a whole or the [Corbyn] project as a whole.

Another Europe were earliest off the ground and, despite their Green-adjacent roots and general pluralism, would remain the biggest organisation dedicated to influencing the Labour Party, with other organisations – including the People's Vote campaign itself – realising that factionally and organisationally, they were simply better placed to influence the party under Corbyn. This being said, Another Europe was far from the only game in town, and there were plenty of organisations more overtly tied to the centre and right of the party.

In August 2017, making the most of the political oxygen that the election earlier that summer had allowed, MPs Heidi Alexander and Alison McGovern (now, respectively, Transport Secretary and Housing Minister) set up the Labour Campaign for the Single Market, which was, fairly self-explanatorily, a campaign to make staying in the single market Labour policy as part of any Brexit deal. In a statement published in *The Observer* and signed by numerous Labour MPs, peers and other elected officials, all of the centre or right of the party – including current Cabinet secretaries Wes Streeting, Bridget Phillipson, Darren Jones, Pat McFadden and Peter Kyle, former party leader Neil Kinnock and future Change UK founding

MPs Chuka Umunna, Gavin Shuker, Luciana Berger and Angela Smith – the campaign argued that 'in the absence of any leadership from the government, our party has a historic opportunity and a duty to set out a clear direction for our country'.[14] They also released a pamphlet titled 'Busting Lexit Myths', a co-production with Open Britain, on which future People's Vote campaign deputy director Francis Grove-White and Mike Galsworthy both get author nods.

As this long list of MPs possibly indicates, the Labour Campaign for the Single Market was a more top-down affair than the other groups outlined here, primarily interested in the positioning (and in publicising the positioning) of MPs rather than in working among the membership. As the list also indicates, the campaign was a project of the right of the Labour Party – Alison McGovern, one of the co-chairs, was also chair of the Blairite campaign group Progress from 2015 – at a time when these distinctions really mattered. These were the people Another Europe and Love Socialism were attempting to avoid being lumped in with in the eyes of the leadership, despite their shared aims.

A few months after the Labour Campaign for the Single Market's launch, Andrew Lewin – then an ordinary party member, since July 2024 the MP for Welwyn Hatfield – set up Remain Labour. While, he says, there 'were people involved … who I really like and admire' in the single market campaign, he felt it was 'overly cautious and wasn't the place that we needed to be if we're going to have any chance'. Open Britain, similarly, were still in a soft-Brexit pose at this juncture.

'We had to demonstrate that Labour members and Labour voters nationally were overwhelmingly on the side of the second referendum, and therefore we had to make a full-throated case for a second referendum and [for] Remain when that came around,' Lewin says of the motivations behind his organisation. 'Because the Labour Party under its [then] leadership wasn't seriously engaging with the question of the second referendum,' he says, 'there was effectively a gap in the market'. Another Europe were focusing to his left, but Lewin's outfit 'worked very well and very constructively with them,' as well as working with what was then Progress and is now Progressive Britain. Lewin describes himself as 'not a factional politician' and says he 'was not attempting to make this about the leadership'.

Lewin was not the only person thinking along these lines. Mike Buckley – a Labour member whose career in international development had, he says, fostered in him an 'internationalist' outlook – felt that 'in the Labour Party' the debate around Brexit 'was stuck'.

'If you were pro-Brexit, or wanting to pretend that you were, then you were sided with the leadership,' he recalls.

> [The] inverse of that is, if you were pro-leadership, you pretty much had to decide that you were pro-Brexit or at least accepted it … and if you were anti-Brexit, you had to side with the right of the party, as in Chuka Umunna, that cohort of people. And that was not helpful in terms of the party having a debate on what [Labour's] Brexit policy was going to be.

Dispirited by this state of affairs, he set up what was to become Labour for a People's Vote in early 2018. 'In retrospect it would have been better to call it something else to differentiate from the People's Vote campaign,' Buckley admits. As one former staffer said, 'We very much saw the Labour Party as the better vehicle to get a People's Vote on the agenda' and didn't seek affiliation with the broader People's Vote campaign.

While Lewin's organisation remained something of a one-man band, Labour for a People's Vote secured funding, hired staff and, like Another Europe, had organisers working around the country – although Another Europe were a 'slightly more well-organised and well-oiled unit than we were,' one former Labour for a People's Vote staffer admitted.

The group spent their time working with the membership and lobbying MPs. Buckley recalls that he would regularly speak to 'senior MPs' who were 'concerned about it and wanted to stave off the worst outcome, which is what we ended up with'. Most of these MPs, Buckley notes, are 'now running the country'.

Like Lewin's Remain Labour, Labour for a People's Vote were non-factional, trying to get away from what they saw as overly charged internal party dynamics. However, factional ick aside, they saw the coalition they wanted to mobilise as being the left and soft left but with slightly more focus on the latter. As one former staffer told me, their 'closest tie to any factional group' in the party was to the soft-left group Open Labour. 'We did also have quite a few prominent Momentum members who got involved with both us and Another Europe,' the staffer notes, adding that 'Laura Parker was quite keen to support us'.

Along with Another Europe and Remain Labour, Buckley's organisation contributed to efforts to push through pro-second referendum policy at Labour's annual conference in 2018 and 2019, which will be discussed in the next chapter. But, after a time, in what is a common trope in this book, Buckley remembers that 'we got to a point where we got the support we were going to get and other MPs didn't want to talk to us, or didn't share our view, or whatever'. And when the organisation hit that point, they had

> kind of run out of things to say, because we didn't have enough votes in Parliament to get where we wanted to get. So, the debate kind of got stuck, because we were making the same points over and over again and it was just – we were spinning our wheels a bit.

Buckley draws several parallels with the People's Vote campaign itself, saying that like the larger organisation, 'we had a lot of success and then it just never coalesced into what it needed to'.

If you are thinking that Labour for a People's Vote and Another Europe were tapping (or attempting to tap) into quite a similar coalition, you would be right. Not everyone in the space, however, was on board with the second referendum proposal. Neal Lawson is executive director of the soft-left think tank Compass, a group that normally sits quite naturally alongside Open Labour, Another Europe is Possible and Love Socialism Hate Brexit in terms of its political positioning and place within the Labour ecosystem: pluralist, interested in radical policies but historically less so in radical faction fighting. Despite a membership that was heavily supportive of a new referendum, however, Lawson had significant doubts about the post-referendum anti-Brexit campaigns and the organisation ultimately did not take a position on a second vote.

Lawson's politics are, he says, fundamentally democratic; he might not have liked the way the vote had happened or its outcome, but it was what it was. He also became, he says, 'increasingly despairing' of the attitude towards Leave voters evinced by many involved with the second referendum campaign. 'There were legitimate left-wing reasons to question the EU,' he says, specifically citing the handling of the Greek crisis, but Lawson felt that 'too many of the second referendum lot' responded to criticisms of the EU, or to Leave voters in general, at a level that could be boiled down to 'shut up, shut up, you're stupid'. Accordingly, he felt that he 'didn't want Compass to be a part of that'. He has time and praise for Another Europe ('they were proposing a more positive agenda for what a more radical Europe' might look like) and doesn't share Schneider's view of them as a front organisation. However, he doesn't dispute that the Brexit issue became 'a plaything of the internal politics of factions in the Labour Party'.

'The Blairites,' Lawson reckoned, had a dual purpose in pursuing anti-Brexit campaigning: 'to game out whether you could start a new party' and to ascertain 'whether you could use it in order to destabilise Corbyn'. He also viewed the issue through a class lens. 'Personally, I mean, clearly, I live in a fucking nice flat in Blackfriars and I'm not working class anymore,' Lawson says, speaking to me at his nice flat in Blackfriars, 'but I was, I very firmly was, and I really felt for me, there was something [with Brexit] – my class is saying something. So, there's a whole load of political, personal and Compass reasons why I was really sceptical about all of that second referendum stuff.'

One person with, in the aftermath of the referendum, an uncommonly good view of what was happening, both within the leadership of the Labour Party and the faction that controlled it, was Laura Parker. Having spent much of her adult life – seventeen years, to be precise – abroad, Parker had briefly been a Labour member in 2011 under Ed Miliband, which she found to be a 'stultifyingly dull and unexciting experience'. She went abroad again and her membership lapsed, but in 2015 she was back in the UK and, thanks to the election of Jeremy Corbyn, back in the Labour Party. Starting from 2016 – shortly before the referendum, in fact – she was not just a member but working for the party as Corbyn's private secretary.

Unlike really quite a lot of people who got stuck into the referendum process and aftermath, Parker had a very good understanding of the EU. She had previously worked, she explains, 'for the European Commission … I was the pre-accession social policy adviser to the European Commission delegation in Bulgaria in the run-up to Bulgaria's accession' and was 'responsible for two chapters in the accession negotiation of Bulgaria for a brief-ish amount of time'. Because of this experience, she says, 'I did have a much better understanding, I think, than many pro-Remain people about the difficulties of getting back in,' given the intense 'complexity' of the accession process even when, as in Bulgaria, it was very much wanted by both the EU and the country joining.

'I don't believe there's a good deal,' Parker explains of her view. 'There's no such thing as a good Brexit.' However, 'relatively speaking, there was a better deal' and so 'I did subscribe to the Jeremy view of not allowing the referendum to further divide the country, which was really his main motivator, and to the idea that we would have to try to push the government to get the best deal that was possible'. However, while to her, like everyone in the office of the Leader of the Opposition, 'Jeremy becoming Prime Minister was important,' Parker says, 'there were some for whom Jeremy becoming Prime Minister was infinitely more important than Britain's relationship with the EU. I guess I didn't see why we couldn't have both.' It was this attitude that led Parker to involvement with Another Europe.

After the 2017 election, she says, debates over Brexit 'started to become a testier issue within the party'. 'It was definitely, for some people, a vehicle for attacking Corbyn.' She adds, 'I'm not suggesting those people were not actually very committed to being in the EU. They definitely were. But it could have been a referendum on something different, and they would have used it the same [way].' Additionally, in this post-election period, 'some of the levels of EU illiteracy were falling away'.

Parker came to support a new referendum 'relatively late, because I did believe in wanting to exhaust the possibilities of trying to get a better deal'. She explains that she 'moved towards it as other possibilities fell away, including just the basic possibility of Parliament ever bloody well agreeing anything'.

As first Corbyn's political secretary and then a senior figure within Momentum, but with a clear affiliation throughout – namely, a new vote – Parker would have a front-row seat to the Labour left's often uncomradely deliberations over the leadership's stance on a new referendum. Perhaps the most heightened moment of this process took place in Liverpool, in the autumn of 2018.

CHAPTER 10

AT LABOUR CONFERENCE, 2018

The shift that had taken place after the 2017 election came too late for the second referendum and general anti-Brexit campaigners to do serious organising around Labour's 2017 conference in the autumn. 'Momentum basically helped the leadership shut down debate on Brexit' at that conference, Laura Parker remembers, which she thought was 'a bad idea. You should not shut down the debate.' To her view, the 'genie cannot be put back in this bottle. The vast majority of Labour Party members were pro-Remain. They remain pro-Remain. That doesn't mean they're anti-Corbyn.' There had been, however, a 'tightening of the circle' and some 'hardening of views' around Corbyn, Parker says, with a more rigid, Lexit-y mindset developing as 2017 turned into 2018 and campaigns for and against Brexit began to kick up a gear.

It was against this mindset, determined not to let the opportunity pass them by for the second year running, that the, by then relatively massed, second referendum forces set themselves to organising in the run-up to the party's 2018 conference. As mentioned, they were in a good position to do so because of the leadership's (in Labour Party terms, comparatively rare) belief in member democracy. As McDonnell put it, to the leadership's view,

> our job was to manage the conference in a way which actually did allow people to have a thorough and proper debate and engage with the delegates again. Under New Labour the conference had been downgraded almost to a spectator sport. So, all our principles were about reclaiming conference as a member-led operation and a member-led process of engagement.[1]

Over the spring and summer of 2018, Another Europe worked furiously at a CLP level. 'We phone-banked every CLP in the country … we really went for it and we did very, very well,' says Chessum. In this period, Chessum also had his first, and to date only, meeting with Keir Starmer, in a cafe by Euston Station, to discuss the motion Another Europe was putting to conference. The then shadow Brexit Secretary was, he recalls, 'extremely non-committal about the whole thing … He gave the impression of somebody who was hedging his bets.'

While Another Europe were leading the effort, they weren't alone. For our Future's Sake was hard at work on the same project and even built an app for conference-goers. 'We were quite happy because we, as a student campaign, built this app that was downloaded by thousands of delegates, one thousand users in two days, at the same time as the official Tory party conference that was just leaking personal data,' one FFS staffer recalls.

'There's a version of history that [says it] was all down to Another Europe is Possible,' Tom Baldwin says, 'but I think winning that vote at the Labour Party conference was down to a lot of people, including not only Michael Chessum but also the brilliant Eloise Todd at Best for Britain, the FFS crew and John Stolliday.' Stolliday, a former director of Labour's governance and legal unit and long-time party staffer, had come to the campaign in summer 2018. Baldwin says he 'knew his way around conference procedures better than anyone'.

'People were happy for Another Europe to basically be seen as one of the leading groups who were involved in the push to get more People's Vote motions at party conference,' Richard Brooks remembers, 'because it was obviously politically helpful to [be] seen to have a group who was … of the left'.

By the time party conference rolled around in September, the motion to back another referendum had more CLPs supporting it than any motion to party conference ever (this record has since been surpassed by a motion backing the Labour membership's favourite hobby horse, proportional representation).

Motions backed by local parties do not, however, simply go to conference floor to be voted on by delegates. First, they are vetted to ensure they meet technical requirements (a badly formatted motion having proved the Achilles heel of many a factional push) and then, if acceptable, they are grouped into policy areas. These areas are then subject to a priority ballot of delegates on the first day of conference.

If the subject gets enough votes to be considered a priority, it will go through a process called 'compositing', where the relevant parties – delegates, from CLPs, socialist societies or trade unions – will gather to synthesise all the motions grouped under the subject into one master motion, the final text of which, once agreed, will then go forward to a vote on the conference floor. These compositing meetings are normally fairly small affairs; there are not regularly more than a dozen or so relevant delegates and officials haggling over the final text of any one motion. Because of the success of the campaign behind the pro-European motion, however, a huge number of delegates would be attending this compositing meeting. It would be chaired by the relevant shadow Cabinet member, the then shadow Brexit Secretary Sir Keir Starmer.

The compositing meeting that took place at the Labour Party conference in September 2018 has become the stuff of legend, albeit only to a very particular kind of person who pays a lot of attention to internal Labour politics. It started at 6.30 p.m. and some comments were made about wrapping up in time to watch *The Bodyguard*, a BBC TV programme which starred actress Keeley Hawes as what many viewed to be a thinly disguised version of then Home Secretary Amber Rudd. It was on at 9 p.m. The attendees would be there until past midnight and miss the programme.

'If you go into a composite without your own draft composite text, you just get rolled over. So, I negotiated in advance a composite text with the GMB and the TSSA [the two unions who were supportive of the new referendum position],' Chessum remembers, and 'then presented that to the delegates.' The Another Europe spokesperson then took up a position outside the door of the meeting room (which was, for any regular Labour conference attendees reading, upstairs in the ACC). As a non-delegate, he wasn't allowed in.

Patrick Jenkins was a student at the time of the 2018 conference, and as a delegate from his local party, he was allowed in (after graduating in 2019, he would go on to work for Labour for a People's Vote). He remembers that he and other delegates were keenly aware that 'the weight is on our shoulders' as they went in to decide the composite: 'If we come out of this room with a vastly different policy to what we had before, this could, if it's done properly, change the future direction of the country.'

It was, he remembers, 'nerve-racking'. Once they got into the room, the debate was heated.

> It was two different camps, one who'd gone in there who were initially anti-referendum, one who'd gone in there who were massively pro-referendum, with a whole bunch of CLPs behind them and trying to somehow form some wording that would allow Keir Starmer and Jeremy Corbyn to go onto the conference floor the next day and say, 'We've come up with a reasonable compromise.' And to be honest, I don't think we, as the pro-referendum CLP delegates, did enough to push our end.

Andrew Lewin, the chair of Remain Labour, was one of the first delegates to speak: 'I was gently saying to Keir Starmer that we should move a little bit further than he wanted us to do, or the leadership, Jeremy Corbyn, wanted us to do.' Lewin remembers this compositing meeting as 'the moment where there was the greatest political interest in what we were doing' when it came to campaigning for Labour to change its position. 'Half the lobby was camped outside,' he remembers. 'There was serious political interest.'

One former trade union official describes the meeting as 'just utterly bizarre' – but also, interestingly given the members were at odds with the leadership on the issue at hand, as a flowering of Corbynism. The official explains that 'a lot of the delegates were the first wave of new people who joined the Labour Party [around Corbyn's election],' got themselves involved in their CLPs and got themselves elected as conference delegates. 'There's a time lag, isn't there? Because you cannot just join the Labour Party and then in two months' time find yourself at conference – you've got to work your way through the system.'

The audience, the official remembers, threw Starmer: 'I don't think he'd done anything quite like this meeting before.' The shadow Brexit Secretary was 'fine' and 'confident, clear and competent' until 'he started getting responses from the delegates', the union official remembers. 'I think it was then when he realised that the normal rules of engagement didn't apply to this room, because he had people standing up, giving personal testimony about the impact of Brexit on their grandchildren's future and people almost in tears over Brexit.'

'Random CLP people' were 'giving massive speeches' and 'cheering and celebrating each other'; it was, the official says, reminiscent of a self-help group.

> It wasn't like, here's the policy issues that I'm taking forward, I want to see this in the composite. It was like a therapy session for Remainers who had newly joined the Labour Party and hadn't accepted Brexit and didn't want to accept Brexit and thought the Labour Party was going to be able to wind the clock back.

The official went on: 'The CLP delegates weren't prepared to reason or understand the frontbench position or the fact that ultimately there needs to be a compromise.' They remember exasperatedly that the delegates 'spent over half an hour trying to discuss "What's the definition of consensus?"' This also crops up in an article written for party news website LabourList by Fiona O'Farrell, a delegate who was active in Remain Labour, who wrote that delegates 'debated and deliberated in a comradely way' and that they even 'had a conversation about what exactly "consensus" means'.[2] Entertainingly, O'Farrell speaks of this discussion as a sign of the delegates' commitment to working through the matters at hand thoroughly, while the official I spoke to seemed to view it more as a marker of naivety and self-involvement, of failing to understand the parameters of the task.

Whether the end result was a success depends on who you ask. Going in, Chessum was fighting for a motion that backed a new vote – a new vote not just on what kind of Brexit the party wanted but on whether to Brexit at all. He did not get what he wanted. The end text reads, 'Labour must support all options remaining on the table, including campaigning for a public vote. If the Government is confident in negotiating a deal that working people, our economy and communities will benefit from they should not be afraid to put that deal to the public.'[3]

The question of 'what was on the ballot paper' of the mooted referendum was 'left deliberately open' in the final text.[4] Starmer, quoted in Baldwin's biography, says he looked the delegates 'in the eye and said there was only one way to get this over the line,' referring to the more ambiguous wording. 'I told them I knew they wanted the option to Remain and promised that, if they signed off this motion, I would faithfully recognise what everyone in the room knew was the basis on which it had been agreed – I gave them my word.'

Chessum, who suspects the unions were offered concessions by the party (specifically, on open selection of MPs, a very live question in the party at the time) to support the weaker wording, was disappointed with the outcome. Laura Parker was similarly disappointed and recalls doing an interview where she 'said something intemperate about, yeah, all options on the table. Where's the fucking table?' O'Farrell, writing six months on, also struck a slightly disappointed note: 'Many of us had to compromise on the final wording of the motion. We ultimately agreed to the "options on the table" pledge, despite the vast majority of motions in the room having been very clear on their commitment to a referendum on the Brexit deal.'[5]

However, despite not getting exactly what they wanted, the campaigners did not leave empty-handed. The motion was an improvement on the party's previous position and Andrew Lewin did a media round the next morning saying as much. More consequentially still, Starmer's 'word' that he would honour the spirit of the agreed position meant that the compositing meeting set the scene for what has come to be viewed as one of the more quietly crucial moments in recent British politics.

The next day, Keir Starmer addressed the delegates in the main hall and, famously, ad-libbed. He had slipped the new line into his speech, very literally – he had tucked a small, handwritten note into the sheaf of pre-approved pages. He read the signed-off line: 'But if we need to break the impasse, our options must include campaigning for a public vote.' Then he went out on his own to add, 'And nobody is ruling out Remain as an option.'

Tom Baldwin has since written a biography of Starmer, which pays close attention to this moment as a point in Starmer's rise. As the People's Vote campaign's head of comms, he wasn't exactly not paying attention at the time. 'After he says it, he kind of looks quite surprised, because two thirds of conference are on their feet cheering.' Baldwin says Starmer, who even his supporters would not describe as a great natural speaker, 'wasn't used to his oratory doing that'.

Seumas Milne, the left-wing journalist turned communications and strategy chief for Corbyn, 'was seeing all the texts of the speeches,' Tom Baldwin notes, and 'wouldn't have allowed that line in there'. Per Baldwin's biography of Starmer, the politician stepped off stage, 'glowing a little bit' (the words of the man himself) because of how well it was received, to be immediately bollocked by Corbyn's political secretary Amy Jackson.[6] Jackson would later say she viewed the line as politicking in service of Starmer's leadership ambitions.[7]

The line was, in Baldwin's estimation, 'one of the very rare moments in party conferences these days when something real happens'. It wasn't 'a great piece of rhetoric. I mean, the actual sentence is garbled' and has 'verbs missing', but nonetheless it provided 'a moment of real electricity'.

The speech was a relief to O'Farrell. 'It certainly reassured me that both the wording and spirit of the motion would be upheld by our party and parliamentarians,' she wrote. For Luke Myer, the whole affair was ultimately a success – and a vindication of the work of pro-second referendum campaigns. 'It's remarkable,' he says, 'the idea that in a few months you could go from a standing start to convincing the shadow Brexit Secretary to ad-lib policy and have the entire room giving a standing ovation. I think that was a really significant moment.'

Many in the pro-second referendum camp, however, were unconvinced by Starmer's turn. 'I think he was a sincere Remainer,' says Patrick Jenkins, 'particularly obviously during the referendum itself, but I don't know how much he was a sincere supporter of a second referendum.' This question – was it good politics, was it sincere principle, or was it a fortuitous combination of both – has hung over Keir Starmer's career ever since. Baldwin's authorised biography has it as a point of principle, a move made to honour commitments given to the delegates in that marathon session. Oliver Eagleton's sharply critical book on the now Prime Minister, *The Starmer Project*, has it as quite the opposite. Luckily for the man himself, the somewhat unknowable nature of the answer doesn't seem to have done him too much harm.

In a grinding and tortured way, the Labour Party came around to the second referendum by increments over the first half of 2019. It softened with statements in February of that year from Corbyn, saying he would back a new vote to stop no deal. By July, the position of the party was to be supportive of a new vote. It billed itself as the 'party of choice', but this choice was to back a new vote while refraining from backing Remain within that hypothetical vote.[8] It was a confusing position, which would not stave off further argument at the party's 2019 conference.

Pressure from members was one factor; the party's poor performance in the local elections (Labour lost control of six councils) and European elections (Labour lost ten MEPs) that spring was another. The latter was to some people's view the deciding factor. Campaigning within the party, via CLP motions etc., for a change of position 'played a significant role' in the ultimate position, one source told me, but 'without a shadow of a doubt, the thing that really changed them was the elections in both May and June'. John McDonnell is generally viewed as having been a key figure in moving the position: his accounts of his reasoning stress party unity and a desire to stem defections in the run-up to and following the Change UK breakaway in February 2019. If Labour hadn't changed positions, he told the journalist Owen Jones, 'we'd have had more defections. It would have split the Parliamentary Labour Party on a bigger scale – one that maybe we'd never have recovered from.'[9] He similarly told UK in a Changing Europe that getting closer to the People's Vote was, for him, about working to 'steady the ship within our own party and within the PLP [Parliamentary Labour Party]'.[10]

Within the party, this decision (and McDonnell's role in it) remains enduringly controversial – particularly on the left, where people often view it as a capitulation to the liberal elite, which severely damaged Corbyn at the 2019 election. Whatever the impact it had on the election's outcome – and, indeed, whether this whole thing was a good idea or not – shifting the Labour Party's position was arguably the greatest achievement of the broadly construed People's Vote campaign.

PART IV

THE PEOPLE'S VOTE CAMPAIGN

CHAPTER 11

OPEN BRITAIN AND THE FORMATION OF THE PEOPLE'S VOTE CAMPAIGN

Open Britain was the organisation that emerged from the ruins of Britain Stronger in Europe, the referendum's official Remain campaign. It started its new life in August 2016 with a handful of staff. Roland Rudd was chair of the board. Rudd, who is founder and chair of the PR firm FGS Global, had set up his first pro-European organisation, Business for a New Europe, all the way back in 2006. Brother to Tory MP, Home Secretary 2016–18 and supposed inspiration for BBC hit *The Bodyguard* Amber Rudd, he was the treasurer of the Stronger In campaign – although, as is near universally true, he did not have a positive view of how things had been run, viewing the campaign as too cautious and passive. Reportedly, he was 'almost the only person interested' in leading the Open Britain board.[1] Others were watching from the sidelines. 'I did not want to organise anything, but I followed very closely what was being organised,' Alastair Campbell said of this period.[2]

The designated Remain campaign's former chief spokesperson James McGrory, who had started his career spinning for Nick Clegg during his time as Deputy Prime Minister, was in position as CEO of Open Britain.[3] Open Britain was, at that time, advocating for a soft Brexit. As McGrory told *The Guardian* in 2018, 'We couldn't just come out and say we didn't agree with Brexit, because we'd just been beaten and it would have lacked credibility. Second, it wasn't where the country was. And third, there was zero appetite in parliament.'[4] One person involved describes their early post-referendum approach as being 'very soft touch' and involving quite a bit of 'feeling around' for how to proceed because 'they knew politically that they couldn't just come out the gate and deny the referendum'. This reality being understood, however, the source contended that 'Open Britain knew from pretty much the beginning that they were going to form a second referendum campaign, but they needed to warm people up to it'.

Open Britain's past as Britain Stronger in Europe gave it an advantage over other organisations – notably, Best for Britain – in that it retained the Remain campaign's significant amount of data, weighing in at around half a million email addresses, and had an existing (if somewhat scant) infrastructure. However, it was also a distinct reputational disadvantage, owing to the fact that everyone disliked and wanted to separate themselves from an official Remain campaign they regarded as, to use a representative view given earlier by Another Europe's Michael Chessum, 'indescribably shit'. It had something of a toxic brand, particularly among the grassroots. Colin Gordon of Oxford for Europe termed it a 'survivor, dead souls, ghostly entity' that despite its infrastructure was a 'Potemkin organisation'. As Mike Galsworthy put it, 'Open Britain couldn't lead it … because they were still trying to campaign for the single market. Given they were the continuation of Britain Stronger In, many of the grassroots felt betrayed by them'. They were, he said, 'really *persona non grata* with the grassroots'.

On the whole, the organisation flew largely under the radar in the first year of its existence; one staffer recalled that Open Britain spent its early days 'trying to work out what to do with that Stronger In data'. This was the strongest tool in its arsenal and a very compelling resource for fundraising and mobilisation – if you can work out what the most useful end to fundraise for and be mobilised on behalf of is. As Henry Mance reported in his excellent *Financial Times* piece about the break-up of the People's Vote campaign, the organisation 'drifted' and 'Rudd called no board meetings between July 2016 and December 2017'.[5] Open Britain also experienced a tragic setback on New Year's Eve 2017, when the organisation's head of press William Cousins was killed in a helicopter crash along with his family. In the press following his death, Rudd described the 25-year-old Cousins as 'an extraordinary young man who took deep pride in his work'.[6]

The organisation caused a small stir in the 2017 election when it released an 'attack list' of twenty pro-Brexit MPs it aimed to unseat, leading to anti-Brexit Conservatives Anna Soubry, Dominic Grieve and Nicky Morgan distancing themselves from the group. 'This sort of blatant partisanship further divides our country when we must all come together,' wrote future Change UK defector Soubry, providing a fascinating before-the-fall glimpse at just how much things would change over the 2017–19 parliament.[7] Open Britain also worked with the European Movement and Britain for Europe – *The Guardian* estimates the three groups had 600,000 contacts between them – to champion a list of twenty anti-Brexit MPs. However, even for a group with the dubious pedigree Open Britain had, a former staffer recalls that it was only at 'the 2017 election, when suddenly parliamentary arithmetic changed' and everything was 'up in the air that Open Britain then shifted to being a bit bolder in what it was asking for' – an ask which would 'eventually evolve into the People's Vote campaign'.

Open Britain was arguably quite a bit more inert than, say, the street stall-running denizens of Britain for Europe, but it remained the largest organisation in the space (as discussed in the previous chapter, the well-funded Best for Britain didn't want to join forces). As such, when it was agreed that an umbrella People's Vote campaign would be set up, on the face of it, it made sense that Open Britain would be the legal entity around which the campaign was formed. The other organisations we have already met – For our Future's Sake, Our Future Our Choice, Britain for Europe, InFacts, the European Movement, Scientists for Europe and NHS Against Brexit – would be quasi-autonomous but would in most practical ways fall under the control of Open Britain. Mance has described this as a 'makeshift solution' that would prove to be 'hugely damaging'.

McGrory and his colleagues at Open Britain, one person familiar with the formation of the campaign said, 'really did recognise that it was a kind of unique monster they were riding. It was less about controlling activists and shipping [in] people. It had to feel organic. It had to feel democratic and spontaneous.' And the 'structures they created', with autonomy for the different groups and voices for smaller organisations like Galsworthy's,

> encouraged that. But at the same time, it makes it quite difficult to manage that untamed beast, which is what Roland Rudd was worried about, that you just wouldn't be able to manage or control any of these people and they'd break off and do all sorts of random stuff.

No one I spoke to was happy with the governance structure that the People's Vote campaign ended up with, which herded the cats into the same bag but did not stop them from biting each other or bitterly fighting for control of the bag. 'We had a very loose governance structure that relied on trust and mutual understanding of the prize,' Tom Brufatto explains, but this meant that there was 'simultaneously too much governance but also not enough good governance'. The governance of the campaign 'was a mess', said Richard Brooks; Amanda Chetwynd-Cowieson agreed that it was not governed or run properly. There would be, as we will come to discuss, significant fallings out in the People's Vote campaign, exacerbated by the way the organisation was set up. However, there is, across the board, fairly consistent acknowledgement that the structure of the campaign was bad.

Its flawed structure even impacted, one staffer told me,

> those kind of logistical things that maybe weren't hot-button issues like messaging and strategy [but] were always simmering under the surface. There would always be someone saying, 'We need an extra chair in that office because we've just hired someone,' and someone else saying – no, arguing – 'Who's gonna get that chair?' You know, all those small-level office politics. It never did the proper, you know, legal merger that it maybe should have at some point.

Its governance ultimately would not work out for anyone, in that familiar manner where a problem is eminently predictable but all involved assume that it can just be muddled through, borne with and improved upon as things go along. Hindsight, however, is 20/20, and despite a campaign structure variously composed of egos and tweets held together by bits of tape, the People's Vote felt they had, by early 2018, sufficiently constituted themselves. It was past time to introduce themselves to the wider world.

The launch of the People's Vote campaign was held on 15 April 2018 at Electric Ballroom in Camden. The event, as various people in attendance remember, was packed and the atmosphere was good. 'Everybody was rammed in,' remembers one attendee. 'There was, like, no breathing.' One person staffing the event remembers a 'very long queue' outside the venue and that backstage, '[Peter] Mandelson was pawing about.'

The launch event 'was meant to be sort of intimidating for everybody else,' they remember. The campaign wanted to say, 'Look, we're here, we're organised. We're really popular. Look how big this queue goes.' They were pleased with how it went, describing it as 'a very well-organised event. If Open Britain could do anything, it was organise these kind of big-statement PR stunts.'

It was also, they said, the first occasion 'where suddenly you have that combination of politicians, celebrities, Open Britain and the amalgam of however many other micro-organisations that somehow wrangled themselves influence' – something that would come to characterise the People's Vote campaign.

Speaking at the event were Caroline Lucas – who various people I spoke to credited with the invention of the term 'People's Vote' – Chuka Umunna, Anna Soubry and Layla Moran, four politicians of different parties but with views very much of a piece on Europe. The MPs were interviewed by the comedian Andy Parsons. Other speakers we've encountered already included Hugo Dixon and Lara Spirit ('I don't think I spoke. I think I was just eye candy,' reminisced Femi Oluwole). Dixon had, Tim Shipman reported, been added to the roster only due to the fairly intense insistence of Roland Rudd. 'When it was pointed out that there was no value in giving such an obscure figure a speaking slot, Rudd insisted until he got his way,' Shipman wrote.[8] Outside, there was a small pro-Brexit protest, with placards reading 'Newsflash: Remain Lost!' and 'Full Mettle Brexit Now'.

Speaking, eye candy or otherwise, the youth campaigns were, naturally, front and centre. 'We ordered, like, twenty T-shirts with the brand FFS on it,' Amanda Chetwynd-Cowieson remembers. She says there was 'definitely a sense of ... not just like something's launching but like something's starting' in the room that day.

The real headliner, however, was actor Patrick Stewart, who told the roughly 1,200 people gathered that the X-Men character he famously played, Professor Charles Xavier, would have voted Remain. 'Unity, common cause, wellbeing of society and debate were paramount to the belief of this fictional character,' Stewart told the audience.[9] 'It was all very hush hush' beforehand says one staffer working the event, with the names of celebrities tabled to speak kept quiet. 'We wanted it to be a surprise when they actually popped up on stage.'

Certainly, Stewart made an impression. 'I'd be lying if I said my biggest memory from that would be all the politics and not standing next to Patrick Stewart,' said Femi Oluwole. Bashir Ibrahim, who describes himself as 'a massive X-Men fan', also remembers being starstruck by Stewart but was still able to take in the broader atmosphere. 'I remember there was this energy in a room,' which he characterises as being not about stopping Brexit but rather 'at that point it was to say, actually, we're not going to remain voiceless in years [to come]'.

The event would prove consequential for Ibrahim; at the time he was working in international development and doing comms- and PR-type work on a freelance basis. He 'stayed behind to network' after the launch and ended up talking to various people already working on the campaign, notably Will Dry of OFOC. He remembers Dry saying they would have some opportunities coming up on the campaign and saying, 'Why don't you ping over your CV?' Ibrahim proceeded to do so. 'They liked the look of it and invited me to a place I'd only heard about, hadn't been to, called Millbank Tower. I go to Millbank Tower and have a quick chat. And the conversation ended with "Can you start on Monday?"' To this, Ibrahim had 'the most typical, Europhile answer, which was "I'm going to Paris for the weekend. I'm back on Monday, I can start on Tuesday?"' This he duly did.

'Looking back now at it,' says Ed Shackle, who was by the time of the launch working for OFOC, it 'was a very sort of London crowd'. He remembers that 'at that point I hadn't met anyone who thought it was a bad idea, so it felt like we had this real wave of everyone was with us'. However, he quickly clocked that he may have been in something of a bubble: 'I remember looking on the news that evening and being disappointed that it wasn't a bigger thing on the news. And that was probably the first time that I got the realisation [that] actually, at that point, it was still fairly fringe.'

As start points go, it was pretty low-key. The launch was well run and garnered some coverage and some attention, but there was nothing that would indicate that the drive for a new referendum would become a key animating force of British politics in the years to come, let alone one which would ultimately be policy (in slightly differing formats) for Labour, the Greens, the Scottish National Party and the Liberal Democrats.

By his own account, the first person to have a People's Vote email address was Tom Baldwin. Having been a *Times* journalist, he'd switched over in 2010 to become Ed Miliband's head of communications. By early 2018 he'd just finished writing a book called *Ctrl Alt Delete* about the media's relationship to politics. The book 'might have been vaguely relevant to the task in hand,' says Baldwin, but mostly he thinks, 'I suppose I was just available.' As discussed, whether you're a seasoned Westminster operative or the host of *Single Minded Rejoiners*, a common cause of heavy involvement in the anti-Brexit movement is being at a bit of a loose end. Baldwin's fellow former Labour spinner Alastair Campbell also became more active at this point, saying, 'Once the People's Vote campaign was up and running, I got very involved, on a day-to-day basis.'[10] He reckoned they were in with a chance: 'I felt it was winnable'.

'You could suddenly see just the slightest hope of a path which would take you out of the chaos and break the stalemate with a new referendum, which could actually be a healing, positive thing,' says Baldwin of his reasoning behind joining up in 2018. 'Even so,' he says, 'when I joined I remember having to clarify our objectives. I said, "Are we fighting for the best possible Brexit, or are we fighting for a new referendum which could stop Brexit?" And I was told, "The latter."'

According to some, Baldwin was essentially smuggled into the organisation by Peter Mandelson and Alastair Campbell, through one of the many holes its patchy governance created. Baldwin's close relationship (and even physical resemblance) to Campbell was often remarked upon. 'Tom and Alastair to some degree may as well be the same person,' one People's Vote staffer told me, adding that 'there used to be a joke that Tom was like Alastair Campbell on a budget'.

Baldwin was paid via a body called the Joint Media Unit (JMU), which some viewed as at a necessary distance from Open Britain and some thought was essentially a Trojan Horse for the ex-New Labour set. To Tom Brufatto's view, the JMU 'had the effect of disrupting the structure of the campaign'.

Despite Baldwin and McGrory having been opposite numbers during their time working for, respectively, the Deputy Prime Minister and the Leader of the Opposition, they quickly forged a close working relationship. Most people I interviewed about the duo's time at the People's Vote campaign referred to them almost as a single entity and certainly, on all substantive issues, as being of one mind. They wanted message discipline and a campaign that didn't seem too Remain-y, and they were supposedly, plenty at the grassroots will say, somewhere between dismissive and hostile towards the grassroots campaigns. 'It felt very much like they were paying us lip service,' said Sue Wilson of Bremain in Spain about the People's Vote operation. 'They didn't want to offend the grassroots of the campaign, but they weren't exactly encouraging us or welcoming us in.'

CHAPTER 12

STUNTS, PRESS AND POLLING

Launched, and with a chair and head of communications only somewhat controversially in place, the first big, unified stunt the groups would connect to carry out would take place at Labour Live. This was a festival thrown by the Labour Party in June 2018. The year prior, Jeremy Corbyn had appeared at Glastonbury Festival, at what people generally acknowledge to be the peak of his popularity, to a rapturous response from the audience. Labour Live was designed to channel and build on that popularity but was widely regarded as an expensive failure. Baldwin describes it as 'this vainglorious summer festival thing that Corbyn wasted a million pounds on'. It certainly didn't help that the youth campaigners of the People's Vote campaign were planning to unveil a massive banner in the middle of Corbyn's speech.

They had, Chetwynd-Cowieson remembers, done a dry run the night before. 'We said to Will Dry, oh, can you book a pub,' so the twelve people involved could hold up the banner to make sure everything worked logistically. 'We'll just get everyone together and we'll just run them through the plan and then everyone have a drink, whatever. So Will, with all of his political nous, booked the downstairs bit of the Red Lion in Westminster.' The banner was 'massive', Chetwynd-Cowieson remembers, something like two by twenty metres (she still has it, folded up somewhere in her flat).

One participant remembers feeling 'scared' and nervous beforehand, stressing that everyone was taking it 'really seriously'. 'We went full-on military about it,' says Chetwynd-Cowieson, who remembers arranging everyone to go in in pairs. ('Don't hang out with each other ahead of time, because it will just be too obvious.')

'I was walking in' with Brooks, Chetwynd-Cowieson remembers, and 'Len McCluskey just walks up beside me. And he was like, "Oh, you guys going to Labour Live? And I was like, yeah."' The then Unite general secretary and key Corbyn ally was chatty, asking them:

> 'What are you both looking forward to?' And in my head, I was like, 'Oh my God.' And then we got to the front gate of it and it was like, bag check and security. And Len had a bag and … the people who were doing security were obviously a bit bowled over that it was him. So they were just, like, chatting to him. So I just opened my bag, and they were like, 'Yeah, fine!' I shut that and ran.

Chetwynd-Cowieson remembers the event itself as being 'only really half full'. In the account given by Patrick Maguire and Gabriel Pogrund in their book *Left Out*, some of the acts 'played to crowds which were in places only two-deep'.[1] When Corbyn got on stage to speak, in the crowd the well-drilled young activists unveiled the banner, which read 'Stop Backing Brexit', a slogan they also began chanting. Corbyn paused, seemingly uncertain how to proceed. The campaigners were fairly swiftly ejected, but they felt the intervention had been a success. People further up the chain thought so too.

As Tom Baldwin remembers:

> Corbyn, who thought he had a monopoly on young people and grassroots direct action, didn't really know what to do with a demonstration against him. He had this sort of puzzled expression, saying, 'This is not how the world's meant to be.' He's usually the one who heckles; he's the one who gets the loudspeaker. He's the one who does the demo.

The stunt, Baldwin thought, was a real success: 'It was very insurgent and just what the campaign needed, because it energised everything. What had been a rather narrow, stale, Westminster corridor-type thing suddenly felt like it was doing naughty things and we were getting in people's faces.'

Labour Live would be the first, but definitely not the last, of the stunts that the People's Vote campaign did. Their logic was quite similar to that of Madeleina Kay: if you give the press an image, they will run it. It existed alongside, almost in competition with, the activities of Kay and her ilk: if we don't provide the image, someone else will. 'I think we were definitely just trying to get into the pitch as much as possible,' says Richard

Brooks of FFS, and 'that meant being quite reactive' and doing 'quite punchy stunts'.

'It's one of those things that you learn' about the British press, Charlie Atkins says. 'If you can get young people and a photo … especially for something where most of the debates are arguments [in the House of Commons] or votes on an amendment or something, they would always just take young people doing something.'

He goes on: 'We'd do stuff that you think was not necessarily that big. And it would get all over the place. Like we did when Boris Johnson prorogued Parliament, I think it was, we just held a big banner up.' Their banner read 'This is not a normal thing' and was held up by a group of around ten young people. Images of it went 'all over the place,' Atkins remembers.

Sometimes it would just be protesting. One former OFOC staffer remembers protesting at Chequers: 'Chequers was such a big part of the Brexit years.' Or it would be fairly simple visuals. One People's Vote staffer remembers participating in stunts themed around both a 'blindfold Brexit' (where blindfolded activists gathered in Parliament Square) and a 'Brexit car crash'. Another recalls a stunt 'with bin bags and rats … we were gonna say there was gonna be a load of rats because of Brexit.' As the staffer recalls, they took plastic rats and 'stacked them all outside one of the government buildings'. Often, however, far more elaborate events were planned.

After having some success with a fairly simple 'People's Boat' stunt – 'It went properly viral,' one person on board remembers, adding, 'It was the illustration to the Brexit story on the six and ten o'clock news' – that just involved sailing down the Thames, the young staff of the campaign hit upon another mission: 'We were trying to hire the world's biggest rubber duck.'

There was a political reasoning and even a history behind the duck plan. Quite a few people on the campaign were Labour Party members, among them a former volunteer for Yvette Cooper's 2015 leadership campaign, who recalled the now Foreign Secretary having made a pledge not to 'duck the fight' if elected. 'She did all these graphics … "If I was leader I wouldn't duck this fight," and it became a meme on Twitter,' they remember, with people joking about fighting ducks. The People's Vote thought they might reuse this messaging to go after Jeremy Corbyn, mocking up banners to be waved alongside the duck that said, 'Jeremy, don't duck this fight', 'For duck's sake, Jeremy' and 'Stop ducking backing Brexit'.

A proposal document was put together for the stunt, the introduction of which opens with 'Jeremy Corbyn has been avoiding Brexit for too long. Therefore,' it continues,

> we are planning to float a giant duck down the Thames in protest at him 'ducking' the issue. As with our boat stunt, the duck will float down past Parliament and down as many laps as possible while the press is situated on Westminster Bridge. The boat pulling the stunt will be full of young Labour members, while the barge itself will also carry team members holding banners.

The boat owner who they'd hired for their first 'People's Boat' stunt had kindly agreed to waive the fee.

Sadly, events overtook the giant duck and it never came to pass. The idea was eventually recycled in a different (specifically, smaller) format, however. During the 2019 Conservative leadership race, the campaign dumped hundreds of regular-sized, bath-appropriate ducks outside Boris Johnson's campaign headquarters. Along with a man in a Boris Johnson mask to pelt with ducks, they had a sign reading 'Stop ducking the Brexit reality'.

It wasn't just the People's Vote campaign, either. Best for Britain got in on the stunts too. 'We had this big "Stop Brexit" red button campaign,' then Best for Britain staffer Flo Hutchings remembers. Part stunt and part advertising campaign (but, I suppose, aren't they all?), the September 2018 gimmick centred around an enormous button with 'Stop' marked on it. Discussing the button, Hutchings notes that 'there was a lot of money going into these campaigns' but 'there wasn't always a clear idea of how best to spend the money'. Of the button, then COO Naomi Smith said, 'I mean, it was a terrible campaign. None of the staff, myself included, thought it was a good idea.' She explains that it

> was taken to the Labour Party conference in Liverpool, September or October 2018. [We'll] get people to just walk past and say, let's hit stop, let's hit pause on Brexit. And it broke and had jaggedy edges and was genuinely dangerous by the end because of so many people jumping on it.

Another Best for Britain stunt involved, Hutchings remembers, 'sending a bin lorry round the red wall'. This was in spring of 2019, so the term 'red wall' – born in the flames of the 2019 election – was yet to come into popular understanding. According to Best for Britain's Twitter account, the bin lorry, with a slogan on the side reading 'Brexit is rubbish', went on a 'tour of the north west and Yorkshire'.[2]

One of the People's Vote campaign's more ambitious stunts happened under the auspices of the 'Farmers for a People's Vote' group. For the launch of that organisation, in August 2019, the People's Vote campaign brought a number of live sheep down Whitehall – and particularly past the Cabinet Office, where no-deal preparations were taking place – to draw attention to the threat to farming from a no-deal Brexit.

Antony So, who was involved in setting up Farmers for a People's Vote campaign, recalled, 'The amount of paperwork that Westminster Council demanded in order to bring in live sheep to Whitehall, you would not believe.'

'That was very typical [of the People's Vote campaign],' one staffer involved recalled. 'Find something visual, do a stunt, invite the press.'

A frequent complaint from those unhappy with Baldwin and McGrory – undeniably creatures of the newsroom and the press office – was that they overly focused on the press, to the detriment of other organising. 'It felt like there was an active scepticism of anything to do with field operations,' Tom Brufatto remembered. 'Lots of them were comms people that had always operated in the comms way,' and their thinking, to his view, was that 'you don't need much else, right? Air war above all else, was my perception of their view.' Another staffer echoed this sentiment, saying that the People's Vote campaign 'essentially ran like a press office that had taken over an organisation'.

One of the big ways the campaign both communicated and fundraised was through frequent emails to the many people on its email list. I spoke to one comms team staffer about the campaign's fundraising emails. The emails were, they say, 'aimed at people who saw it as a monumental issue that they wanted to do something about'. They were for fundraising, 'but it was also our way of getting the messaging out to supporters'. The core message 'changed a bit' over time. 'When we got to a position where we were clearly very deadlocked' in Parliament, then the message 'was very much the only way through this mess is another People's Vote, or it was essentially another vote on the final deal'.

They did 'a lot of segmentation' when sending out emails. In terms of raising money, 'the ask was variable,' the staffer says, and a 'portion of the emails would be aimed at people who'd never donated, so it'd be a low ask'. Not so for everyone, however: 'Some of the people who donated, they would give maybe even like a thousand pounds an email … I'm pretty sure the top aims were pretty high, and we could get them.'

Baldwin praised the people who put together the emails as being 'very good at it'. The financials – Henry Mance reported that the campaign was at one point pulling in £100,000 a week via email donations alone – would seem to bear this out.

'We wouldn't allow anything that made us look like we were a Remain campaign or about just opposing all forms of Brexit,' Baldwin explains of their email strategy.

> We tried to make them a call to action – seizing on something that was in the news that day. You know, have you heard what's happened? This is urgent. And bless them, the people were giving us money. And there are some people who gave us £5 or £50 or £100 every time we asked. They were magnificent and I feel awful that we let them all down. A lot of people gave us a lot of money individually, people that probably couldn't afford it … we got really good letters from some of them, heartbreaking letters, about, you know, this big moment in their life, about what sort of country they lived in.

The campaign would often send out emails under the names of second-referendum supporting politicians. One comms staffer I spoke to remembers that David Lammy was a particular pull. Sending out these emails, however, also meant that people could write back. Communication is a two-way street.

I spoke to one member of the People's Vote team whose job, in part, involved keeping an eye on the inbox as people responded or wrote in with their own views. 'The emails the campaign got from members of the public were a mixed bag, pretty much a fifty-fifty split,' they remember, between supporters and opponents. Both sides of the debate were 'really passionate', with 'pro-Europeans saying that in order to advance democracy, we should have a second vote to be absolutely sure of the direction the country was travelling in. Pro-Brexit people would email the campaign basically saying they thought we were a bunch of anti-democratic fascists.'

'One end of the extreme was the increase of racist hate email people thought they were sending to Chuka Umunna and Sadiq Khan whenever the campaign sent out a message in their names,' they remember.

> These would actually land in the People's Vote inbox and we would have to sift through the incoming emails to identify if there was anything so shocking that we had to report it to the police, and I think on one or two occasions we did have to do that. On the other end of the extreme, there was the time People's Vote had to call off a rally at short notice because it would have clashed with a fundraiser by Great Ormond Street Hospital. Shockingly, *some of our own supporters* were writing in to the campaign saying didn't [Great Ormond Street] understand that opposing Brexit was more important than raising money for sick children, and it was the hospital who should be cancelling their event, not us?

This is, somehow, not the only incident of the Brexit culture war finding its way to the doors of Great Ormond Street Children's Hospital. In October 2018, a man whose eleven-year-old stepson was being treated at the hospital tweeted that the child was 'gutted' to miss the People's Vote march, accompanied by a picture of his stepson in his hospital bed with an EU flag. Stewart Jackson, until 2017 the Tory MP for Peterborough, responded to the picture, tweeting, 'What a pathetic cretin.' Then Tory MP Heidi Allen called Jackson 'pathetic, unkind and a nasty man' in response.[3]

The war on children's hospitals aside, a staffer for a People's Vote-supporting MP discussed a similar experience:

> One of the things I had to do in that job was manage the fucking MP inbox. And the amount of abuse, the sheer weight of it. You get all the people on the right writing and saying that you're traitors, and then you get all the people on the left writing in and saying that you're traitors.

It all, they said, 'dog piled, and so MPs were literally driven mad. The abuse is pretty bad now, but at that point it was really fever pitch.' Lloyd Russell-Moyle, an MP at the time and one very active in the push for a new referendum via Love Socialism Hate Brexit, takes a slightly different view. From his perspective, people 'protesting, shouting, screaming' was overall a very good thing. 'You had a lot of very wet MPs who complained about how horrible it was. I mean, I had bullets through my door and I was attacked in the street, but broadly it was great. Because people were involved in politics,' he says.

As a prominent campaigner, Femi Oluwole was also cognisant of the abuse and risks he faced. 'I was getting death threats on a regular basis,' he says.

> So much so that the Metropolitan Police had my number on a special list. If I called them, it was automatically flashing lights.

> And I'd done the maths in my head, all the risk factors that were associated with Jo Cox applied to me, other than being a woman, and she was killed by a white supremacist, so I've got one on top of that. I was getting regular death threats and so I did the maths … I acted on the basis that I probably might not make it through, but I've done the maths that if the British Medical Association is saying that a no-deal Brexit, which was the policy of people like Nigel Farage and Boris Johnson at several points, would be a catastrophe for the NHS [and] would make us more vulnerable to deadly pandemics. That was their 2018 analysis, that that would cost thousands of lives, and I'm only one guy, so let's go.

Email donations were a significant revenue stream, but separate donations from wealthy individuals were also important to the campaign. The largest single donation came from Julian Dunkerton, the millionaire owner of clothing giant Superdry, and Mance reports that it was arranged under the auspices of Alastair Campbell. Dunkerton gave the campaign £1 million, with a string attached: it could only be spent on polling. He publicly announced the gift in August 2018, saying, 'I've got a good instinct for when a mood is going to change and we're in one of those moments now.'[4] He would, he said, 'be paying for one of the most detailed public polling exercises ever undertaken by a campaign, so more of us have the confidence to demand the democratic right for our voices to be heard.'[5]

Opinion is, it is fair to say, divided on whether this caveat was good for the campaign. One person I spoke to described it as a 'massive, massive outlier' in terms of amount of money spent on polling in a UK politics context. British politics is famously cheap; by this person's estimate, 'the Labour Party's polling budget in [the 2024 election] was probably higher than any party's polling budget in any election ever and [the People's Vote campaign's] was certainly significantly higher than that'. It was a truly huge amount of money to spend on polling.

Despite the intensive surveys – one person I interviewed described the organisation as 'awash with MRPs' following Dunkerton's donation; another said that 'every fucking week it was a new poll from YouGov' – plenty were unconvinced of its merits as a grand tool of persuasion. In one person's reckoning, it was not

> really adding very much value at all. It was all saying exactly the same thing, which is, the country had sort of just about slipped from fifty-two to forty-eight one way, to fifty-two to forty-eight the other way. But most of the time, people didn't really think there should be a referendum, because we [had] just had one.

People were tired of hearing about Brexit, in some cases literally. In a study on Brexit's impact on people's personal lives, academics Katherine Davies and Adam Carter documented one of their participants literally falling asleep in the time they'd set aside to catch up on news about the process, an example which, they argue, 'epitomises the challenge of keeping informed about Brexit among the other challenges of day-to-day life in the UK. Everyday life can be exhausting, and Brexit exacerbates this slog.'[6]

Journalist Stephen Bush says that if you spend any time talking to people involved in running UK political parties, 'they will complain about some of the mad ideas that donors have for how their money is best spent'. Good political operations can shut this down, but, in his assessment, 'one of the problems the pro-European campaign had' was that 'almost by definition' it had 'no leader. It has no one who can look across the table at any of these donors and go, I'm sorry, this is not a good way to spend your money.' Again, we come back to the governance problems inherent in the setup of the People's Vote. If no one's quite certain where the buck stops, you might end up spending a million quid on polling. Or trying to make it look like you had. 'An enormous amount of time,' one staffer told me, 'went into trying to work out whether there was stuff we could say was polling that wasn't', in order to get around Dunkerton's edict. They deemed the situation 'ludicrous'.

Not everyone, however, was so critical. Bashir Ibrahim's response to the idea that too much money was poured into it is to remark that 'hindsight is a beautiful thing'. He asserts that the polling played a valuable role. 'We needed to show people that this was a viable option,' he says, and extensive polling, consistently written up in the press, was a way to show that to both politicians and the public. To his view, 'Polling played a very vital role in the People's Vote campaign strategy, and I think anyone else who says it didn't is not being honest.'

Tom Baldwin is of the view that polling of Labour members was 'very, very influential' in shifting the Labour leadership's position on a new vote. As he ultimately regards this position change as among the great triumphs of the second referendum campaign, one can infer that he thinks the group's big polling spend was worthwhile.

CHAPTER 13

THE MARCHES

There had been a slew of anti-Brexit marches of one kind or another following the referendum, but it was only after the People's Vote campaign had coalesced in April 2018 that demonstrations in the capital, organised by the newly minted Millbank operation, began to get serious numbers. Their first march was in June 2018, marking two years since the vote to leave, and was estimated at around 100,000 participants.[1]

'Our first march was messy with terrible operation – there was chaos backstage – but also an important breakthrough in lots of ways because it led the news and got us on the pitch,' remembers Tom Baldwin.

> We were smart enough to do it at a weekend when nothing much else was happening politically and we could get lots of people marching through London. I remember seeing the aerial shot of the whole of Whitehall packed with this mass of people surging through and thinking, 'Wow, this is a big moment for us.'

They built on this momentum in October 2018, fresh off their successes at Labour Party conference. The march held on 20 October that year 'exceeded all expectations of both the organisers and police' – so said *The Observer*'s report on it at least, which put the numbers at 'almost 700,000' and termed it 'the biggest outpouring of public opposition to government policy since the anti-Iraq war protest in 2003'.[2] OFOC co-founder Lara Spirit later said she 'literally just burst out crying' when she heard they'd hit the 700,000 figure.[3] These were big, impressive events. 'I worked one where I sat at the top of Portcullis House with a camera just pointing down at Parliament Square and watched all the crowds come in,' says one People's Vote staffer, who describes themselves as having been 'blown away by it all'.

In March 2019 came the 'Put It to the People' march; the People's Vote campaign (via their Twitter account) claimed that there had been a million people at the demonstration, although FullFact put the number at between 312,000 and 400,000. Either way, hundreds of thousands of people flooded through central London. *The Guardian* reported that 200 coaches bused people in from all around the country, including one leaving from the Scottish Highlands on the Friday night, with another departing from Penzance, Cornwall at 3.15 a.m. on the day of the march. Quoted in the piece, James McGrory termed it the 'biggest mass movement in the country'.[4]

The last People's Vote march would take place on 19 October 2019. The organisers again claimed – and it seems were nearer the mark this time, although the BBC puts the figure at 700,000 – that they had gotten a million people out on the streets.[5] That march coincided with a rare sitting Saturday in Parliament, with MPs voting on the Letwin amendment. (The amendment passed, denying Boris Johnson a 'Yes' vote on his deal and pushing approval for Brexit back, in what was one of many keenly felt but ultimately inconsequential victories for the anti-Brexit side.)

The Guardian posted a short video of scenes from the day, providing an insight into both the feeling on the ground and how the media reported it, with a focus on conflict and on the visually interesting or twee. At one point, a man holding a banner reading 'Any Brexit is a pyrrhic Brexit' is repeatedly called a 'traitor' by a counter protester, who he in turn dubs an 'ignorant dick'. Talking to the camera, the anti-Brexit protester says, 'That's what you're up against, isn't it? When you have to try and reason with people like that just says it all. We come out with witty signs; they come out with bluster and bullshit.' Another man interviewed in the video has his face almost entirely covered in 'Bollocks to Brexit' stickers. Two women dance in front of a sign saying 'Middle-aged rave'. A woman with a small dog (they are both wearing Bollocks to Brexit stickers, of course) is asked what her pet makes of Brexit. 'He hates it, he'd prefer to be able to go across the channel whenever he feels like it.' A week and a day later, the ailing campaign would blow up completely, so these are scenes from the end of the line: the October 2019 march can be seen as the last act of the People's Vote campaign.

The marches all took a similar format, winding a path

through central London before ending up in Parliament Square, where the crowds would be addressed by a range of politicians, celebrities and campaigners. At the final rally, after the October 2019 march, Mayor of London Sadiq Khan, who had addressed several of the marches, spoke alongside food writer Delia Smith (in her view, Brexit is a 'dog's dinner').[6] Smith's headliner status – she spoke at more than one of the rallies – was brought up by Ed Shackle as he discussed how OFOC felt the need to try to get younger celebrities and influencers involved. 'I'm a huge Delia Smith fan, don't get me wrong,' he says, but 'she's not gonna get everyone around the country up on their feet.' The March 2019 rally was hosted by Richard Bacon and Mariella Frostrup, and featured speeches from Nicola Sturgeon, Jess Phillips, David Lammy and Dominic Grieve. Amanda Chetwynd-Cowieson remembers getting Sturgeon, then Scottish First Minister, to speak as being a particular coup for the campaign.

Most people I spoke to credit Rachel Kinnock – director of events and visits in Gordon Brown's Downing Street and during Ed Miliband's time as Leader of the Opposition, daughter of former Labour leader Neil Kinnock and former MEP Glenys Kinnock, and sister of serving MP Stephen Kinnock – with the success of the marches on a logistical level. One staffer terms her 'one of the great unsung heroes of the campaign'.

The exact figures for attendance at all of these marches are debated and hard to pin down precisely; you can, however, comfortably say that they were, by the standards of British political demonstrations, very large. A lot of the protest activity thus far discussed in this book – the street stalls and petitions and smaller marches – was basically ignorable for most normal people, even those paying reasonable attention to the news. You can choose not to sign up to an email list, to avoid eye contact with the activists at the anti-Brexit stall on the high street. The marches, however, provided moments when anti-Brexit campaigners – and even more specifically than that, the call for a new referendum – punched through into the true mainstream. One former staffer, who, in the grand anti-Brexit tradition, hadn't attended any protests previously, described them as 'peculiarly jolly. People were clearly really angry and wanted to do something … people were very smiley and there was a sense of urgency, but it didn't feel like a pressure cooker.'

Dorian Lynskey of *Remainiacs* had been to many protests before and liked the atmosphere at the People's Vote marches. He described them as 'incredibly positive', saying that at most protests he'd been to there'd be some stuff he didn't like, an unpleasant edge – an antisemitic banner, a group trying to kick things off – whereas 'there it was incredibly benign. And you could therefore say it was older and middle class and smug and blah, blah, blah, blah, blah, but it was very interesting to have a protest where there was this genuine sort of unity, really not a lot of tension.' Another Europe is Possible, he remembers, ran a large left block, but no one was scowling at each other. It all 'seemed quite upbeat. And it seemed like, oh, there's enough people here that this is a genuine movement.

And it brought together quite a lot of values. It focused quite a lot on values in terms of liberalism and internationalism.' He even liked the speakers – even though, naming no names, he admits that some of them, he felt, were 'kind of, you know, narcissists'.

However, just as the marches were a sincerely useful show of force, they also demonstrated, in a concentrated format, the many tensions between the People's Vote campaign and the grassroots of the anti-Brexit movement. In short, the people who showed up to the marches shared, generally speaking, the demographic and the ideological profile of the grassroots, and that was not a great look for the campaign.

'One of our big concerns was always that the marches looked weird,' one staffer recalled. 'I mean, they were always gonna look a bit weird, right? You've got, like, nearly a million people marching to be members of a supernational body, but they didn't look or reflect the population that we were claiming to be able to speak for.'

There were concerted attempts for the marches to be demographically mixed and particularly to feature young people. 'We would, every time, have big arguments about the difference between if we spend this much money in rural Hampshire, we know that we'll get X many people,' one staffer remembered. 'And, yeah, but if we spend that money in universities, then we might get less people, but then at least they might look like the sort of people [we claim to represent].' Hugo Dixon strikes a more phlegmatic note when I ask him about this issue: 'I think you want to have as many people as you can, so I don't think you turn people away' or say 'Oh, I'm sorry, you're white and middle class and you've got a university degree, so you can't come on our march.'

'Lots of the people in our marches', recalls Baldwin,

> weren't just Remainers but 'blue berets with gold stars' Remainers. We were emboldening a network of grassroots organisations always pushing us to be more Remain, even 'revoke'. It's the same dilemma which the Conservative Party has faced, the Labour Party has faced, which is the more you empower an activist base, the less you look like the people which you should be attracting.

This was part of an overall image problem, Baldwin remembers: 'The bigger the marches, the more important the marches became. The more important our fundraising – because we weren't getting big individual donations – the more important our activists became. It meant our image was becoming more and more Remainy.' As a result of this audience capture, 'we were becoming part of a polarisation problem, to which we could or should have been the solution'. As Eloise Todd of Best for Britain put it, 'The big marches, the kind of performative stuff like that … it felt at some points that that was feeding the troops rather than going beyond that,' which she describes as 'a classic concern or challenge of any campaign'. Another senior People's Vote staffer struck a similar note: 'They look good and they get a bit of TV,' but 'our game was about changing MPs' lines, right? And the big marches at the end, did any

MPs switch from the Conservatives to Labour to try and stop a general election? I'm not sure they did do that.'

This demographic might not have been politically ideal, but the pure concentration of hardcore anti-Brexit campaigners meant that these were red-letter days for the EU micro-celebrities. The insular nature of their fame meant that on a normal morning they might not have a problem popping out for some milk, but at a People's Vote march they were as famous as any A-lister. Femi Oluwole recalls, 'Every Remain or anti-Brexit march is always a very peculiar day for me, because it's a day where everybody knows your name, and you walk through a crowd of one hundred thousand, two hundred thousand, seven hundred thousand people and everybody knows your name and shakes your hand.' I can attest to this; I first approached Oluwole for an interview at a Rejoin march. Despite that being many, many times smaller than the marches of 2018 and 2019, I had to join a small queue to talk to him; it had the air of a slightly past-it boy band member appearing at a regional shopping centre, only instead of hordes of teenage girls, his fans were a handful of retirees. Oluwole describes his experience of being an EU micro-celebrity at the marches as 'cool, obviously' but also as high pressure, 'because that's how many people are counting on you to turn the ship around'.

One of the ways the campaign tried to make the marches seem less Europhilic and less, well, weird, was by limiting the presence of European flags. This was policy not just at the marches. As one staffer remembers, 'During that summer in 2019, every event that we did, the European flag was pretty much banned … Union Jacks were handed out to people and we tried to ask activists not to bring European flags.' They were, basically, unsuccessful. 'There was no practical way that they could go up to people and say, remove your beret and put away your European flag,' another staffer recalled. They remember attempting to dilute the presence of the blue flags: 'As a staffer, when we tried to hand out actual small Union flags on Parliament Square, people would literally refuse them. They would say, "No, do you have a European one?"' The reception was poor. 'The instinctive reaction of the ultra-Europeans' to the offer of Union flags was, they remember, '"That's basically a National Front symbol." And I said, "No, it's our flag, don't be afraid of it."' The campaign, they recall, 'really, really, really wanted' lots of 'of red, white and blue' in the crowd, and 'it would have been possibly a little more helpful' to overall perceptions if they'd managed it.

In case you have got this far into the book without realising this yet, the anti-Brexit movement had a cringe problem. 'The optics of the berets … It was like, you know, the older, middle-class, white people,' says then Best for Britain staffer Flo Hutchings. 'It didn't feel very cool, basically, like it lacked a big old cool factor.' At the marches, this lack of cool factor and a tendency to indulge in what can only be termed Remainer cringe-core, was very much on show. After the October 2018 march, the film producer Dominic Minghella infamously tweeted, 'On today's march, I ducked into Pret along with many other People's Voters. It was heaving and chaotic, but we formed genteel queues, laughing – "No, no, after you–" "Do you mind if I just?" – because decent. Because cooperative. Because positive. Because properly British.'[7]

Minghella, who would subsequently make a film titled *We Wants It*, which features Andy Serkis as a Gollum-like Theresa May who craves a deal on Brexit, was roundly mocked for this tweet. According to an article about it in the *Belfast Telegraph*'s opinion pages – the attached photo is a woman in a bEUret – it 'attracted much mirth and ridicule', but it does show, albeit in an exaggerated way, something about how (some) anti-Brexit campaigners thought about themselves and their movement.[8]

Another hub of cringe came with the 'Wooferendum' group, founded by sustainable skiing journalist Daniel Elkan (most recent *Telegraph* article at time of writing: 'The 15 best ski resorts you can reach by train'), which campaigned against Brexit through the lens of dogs.[9] The campaign styled itself as being 'by the dogs, for the people,' with its crowdfunder – which raised almost £8,500 – asserting that 'the people and dogs of this country are not going to roll over and let Brexit happen'.[10] While present at the larger marches, the group also held its own pet protest in early October 2018, which featured 'pee stations' decked out in pictures of Boris Johnson and Nigel Farage for dogs to relieve themselves.

'The Wooferendum was godawful,' Sarah Jones, aka online anti-Brexit personality Sarah Saboteur, says. 'I made a point of not attending "protests" like that because I felt they were so damaging to the campaign. Like that infamous placard about the dog not being able to go skiing post-Brexit because it hasn't got an EU passport.' The sign she's referencing here was made by food writer Felicity Cloake and features an image of her dog Wilf (who she also brought to the protest) crying alongside a flaming pet passport, with the caption, 'You tell him he can't go skiing next year Theresa.' Given a 2023 *Times* article by Cloake titled, 'It's not just the Middletons. I took my own dog skiing. Here's how,' this complaint would seem to be in reasonable earnest.[11]

The group was, to Sarah Jones's view, 'completely out of touch.' She thought that

> stuff like that only helped cement Remain as a position/campaign for privileged rich people, while Leave easily maintained their facade as the campaign for the regular working man. It's funny because they thought basing that protest around dogs would win people over because everyone loves dogs, but it still backfired; so many of the people in charge had no idea how to relate to normal people. It's like they just weren't part of the real world.

It might be fair to note that the Wooferendum, registered on Companies House in Elkan's name, was not affiliated to the People's Vote and that it's unfair to pin this particular crime of cringe on any 'people in charge.' However, given that Alastair Campbell, certainly an influential figure at Millbank, was photographed with his dog at the Wooferendum event, perhaps it is not entirely unfair. Campbell's picture in *The Guardian* was captioned 'Doggy dossiers: the former Labour spin doctor Alastair Campbell with his dog, Skye,' which is, when you think about it, pretty misjudged.[12]

What was, perhaps, in the worst taste of all was the small trend for marchers to wear yellow stars, cross-referencing the stars of the European flag with the stars worn by Jews under Nazi rule. I spoke to one woman who had done this, who explained that she had lost family in the Holocaust and had, in the Brexit years, restored her German citizenship: 'I definitely see myself as more European than British, but I think if your family come here as refugees, as mine did, you never fully integrate.' In the wake of Brexit, she was particularly concerned by xenophobia and abuse directed towards 'anyone who spoke with a "foreign" accent'. As with a lot of people I interviewed in this book, the answer here is the most reasonable explanation of the action – without making the case for it as a particularly good way of persuading people of the benefits of EU membership or a new referendum.

Not everyone looks back on the marches with fondness, however. Mike Buckley reflects that when there were hundreds of thousands marching down The Mall,

> I don't think we realised what it looked like to the rest of the country, and to the rest of the country we just look mad, you know? And I do get that now, and I also get that a lot of people who had rarely voted before, in some cases never voted before, felt … 'I turned up to cast my vote for this and you're trying to take it away,' and I get why that made them angry.

CHAPTER 14

DYNAMICS AT MILLBANK

Many of the young staffers recall the People's Vote campaign being a fairly good social scene. People worked long hours together, got to know each other and formed lasting friendships. The local pub to Millbank Tower was The Grosvenor; as one person who worked on the campaign recalled, there were points when the staff were in there 'like, three, four times a week … there was lots of drinking in this campaign'. (The staff's favoured watering hole would come to play a substantial role in the campaign's final act.) In the office, their anthem was 'Happy Birthday'. 'Any good moment we would sing "Happy Birthday,"' Bashir Ibrahim remembers. 'Even if it wasn't their birthday, if someone did a really good media performance then we'd sing it.'

The office had a football team that would play every week (and is, I understand, still going). It was composed mostly of the younger, more junior staffers, but McGrory and Baldwin would occasionally join. Charlie Atkins remembers Baldwin having a 'very '90s style' of play as a footballer.

The young staff of the People's Vote campaign, by and large, adored James McGrory and Tom Baldwin. It was, as OFOC's Ed Shackle remembers, 'most of our first jobs. We didn't know what we were doing. We were sort of learning on the job … Tom and James were incredibly helpful and friendly.' Luke Myer of FFS had a similar, positive impression: 'Like anyone who's worked in comms at a senior level, there's a lot of myths around [Tom Baldwin]. He's not as combative in reality. I found him genuinely very empathetic towards the staff, and that was always his focus throughout.' Several staff I spoke to started at InFacts and moved over to the People's Vote campaign. ('McGrory did have a tendency to quite enjoy stealing staff from InFacts,' one remembered.) Having found InFacts a 'quite hard place to work,' the main campaign was, one said, 'a much nicer working environment' and also one that made more sense to them. They felt there was 'more rationale behind some of the decision-making.'

The general regard wasn't limited to the younger staffers of the People's Vote campaign. Mike Buckley of Labour for a People's Vote described Baldwin as 'very, very capable', while Michael Chessum of Another Europe is Possible said his impression was that the comms director 'played with a straight bat.' A senior staffer noted McGrory's long tenure – having worked for Britain Stronger in Europe, then Open Britain both before and after it joined the People's Vote campaign – describing him as the 'last Japanese soldier on an island sort of thing but without being mad. James is not mad, so that's good.' The staffer added, 'You can basically divide all of the people who were involved into, in the end, mad and not.' I leave readers to make their own appraisals of who falls into which category.

The reviews were not all positive – some people I spoke to took issue with the pair's conduct, viewing them as domineering or bullying. Mike Galsworthy thought that at one point James McGrory was trying to pit him and his Scientists for Europe co-founder Rob Davidson against each other, about which he found himself thinking:

> Fuck you. Fuck you. That was a nasty move. You're trying to play us off against each other. It was really aggressive and manipulative. You know, I'd gotten on with James McGrory well for all of 2017. I found him a bit huffy and puffy and melodramatic at some points, but that was the first time that he was being really aggressive and controlling.

As then Green Party leader Caroline Lucas observed, 'I think the culture over at Millbank Tower, the perception at least from the outside I got was that it was a very macho, rather exclusive operation.'[1]

However, it is worth noting that the more negative views all came from more senior people within the organisation, mostly people like Galsworthy running their own sub-group or people outside the People's Vote campaign observing the dynamic from outside. People in this category would often in turn speak quite pejoratively about the young staff as, essentially, starstruck and manipulable puppets of Baldwin and McGrory. The people who worked *for* the pair, however, tended to be positive, even effusive. I spoke to around a dozen people who did work directly under them, all but one of whom were very positive. The one outlier took a 'pox on all your houses' approach, terming the organisation cliquish and saying that Baldwin and McGrory operated a culture of patronage, though not backing up assertions of any bad behaviour.

All this being understood, I think it is fair to say that the younger staffers held the director and the comms chief in very high regard. Even Galsworthy doesn't see any particular conspiracy or manipulation in the relationship between the two men and the junior staffers: 'McGrory and Baldwin loved them and the staff loved them back. They had very much invested in them and nurtured them.' His is also of the view that the director and comms chief had 'to a degree, created bogeymen slightly outside of them, namely Tom Brufatto and myself and Hugo Dixon' and used this to cement us-v-them loyalties.

A majority of the people who started out their careers on the People's Vote campaign continue to work, in one form or another, in politics. They are aides and MPs and journalists and pollsters and are no doubt influenced by their time there and particularly by Baldwin and McGrory. Having assessed them as good people to work for, it's still fair to wonder whether this influence is completely positive. It's certainly something of which Tom Baldwin is proud, and fairly so. 'I think there's a whole generation of people who cut their teeth in politics as part of that campaign whose influence will be felt for quite a long time,' he told me. But there is, for example, a distinctly

The Thick of It smack to one young staffer's easy reference to a Millbank room they called 'the room of screams', slightly apart from the main office and therefore perfect 'if you wanted to shout at a journalist or something'. While intensely committed, they were also not necessarily modelling the healthiest lifestyles and work–life balances: 'I watched James McGrory smoke like 500 cigarettes on this little patch of fake grass outside Millbank Tower,' another staffer, then in their early twenties, remembers.

One young person who worked for the campaign (and described Baldwin and McGrory as good managers who were 'extremely supportive', noting that they 'elevated the voices of young people' in the workplace) summed up the environment: 'A lot of the young people were… I wouldn't necessarily say [they] worshipped Tom and James but really looked up to them.'

'James especially was so inspiring to young people,' they explain.

> I think he started – he ran Clegg's comms for the coalition government I think at the age of, like, twenty-six. He was really young, and both he and Tom are extremely passionate, you know, political actors, in a way that, at the time, felt amazing, but subsequently, working in politics, I'm like, that is actually really unique, the amount that they cared and invested in the stuff they were doing. And James, especially, I remember being at the pub with him one night in the early days and it was literally like the young people were a kind of flock of sheep listening to him. It was like we were totally enthralled by what

> he was saying. He'd tell us these tales from it … it was the loyalty of it as well. He was like, I would lie down in a road and die for Nick Clegg. You know, you totally believed him. Totally believed him. But it was also— him and Tom were actually very professional, you never felt like you could talk to them about your personal life or whatever.

The odd game of football notwithstanding, it wasn't 'buddy buddy, all in the trenches together, let's share everything about ourselves,' the staffer adds.

As alluded to, if relations between Baldwin and McGrory and the junior staff were good, relations between them and the other heads of organisations were less so. Tom Brufatto, working in Millbank as the chair of Britain for Europe, remembered that with McGrory in particular 'it felt quite confrontational from week one'. Tim Shipman describes the campaign behind the scenes as being a 'bearpit of internecine warfare'.[2] InFacts was suspicious of Open Britain; the Open Britain board members were suspicious of each other; and despite their alignment, the European Movement was sporadically suspicious of Britain for Europe's claims to be the greater hub of activism.

There were, very roughly, two sides: Rudd and Dixon and a loose assortment of some of the more grassroots-aligned organisations versus McGrory and Baldwin and the bulk of the People's Vote staff, who mostly came out of or were aligned to the moderate end of the Labour Party. The difference over strategy could be seen as this: Rudd and co. preferred a more pro-European angle, empowering the grassroots in line with the messaging from InFacts discussed in Chapter 5, while McGrory and co. wanted a more softly-softly approach that focused heavily on winning over moderate Tory MPs and shifting the parliamentary balance.

Tensions weren't just playing out at the senior level. The friction between the youth organisations discussed in Chapter 4 continued. One point of tension was Oluwole's flirtation with standing for Parliament – specifically, with being a candidate at the Peterborough by-election, which took place in June 2019. The seat had been won by Labour from the Conservatives in 2017 – in fact, from Conservative Stewart Jackson, last spotted in our narrative posting 'cretin' under pictures of sick children – but the MP, Fiona Onasanya, had quickly become embroiled in legal issues relating to a speeding incident and her subsequent attempts to avoid punishment. (Her memoir *Snakes and Adders: A Set Up for the Step Up* is revealing and informative, although likely not in the ways that Onasanya intended.) When a recall petition triggered a by-election in May of 2019, Oluwole considered standing as a unity anti-Brexit candidate and had support from the Greens, the Lib Dems and Change UK.[3]

Richard Brooks remembers that Oluwole 'wanted to be a representative of the People's Vote campaign and was using [People's Vote campaign] resources to run as a candidate'. Reading between the lines, Brooks was clearly not supportive of the idea but moderates himself to commenting that it 'would have been a lot of resource' and constituted 'quite a challenging regulatory legal situation' for the People's Vote campaign.

Oluwole reasoned that 'with any political campaign, the scramble is for media attention and to get the message out there as loudly as possible. And what better way than to be one of the politicians that the mainstream media just flocks towards?' He describes his consideration of running for Parliament as being first and foremost about being able to 'get the arguments that I've been making across the country into Parliament'. In the end, however, he decided against it, discussing his decision not to run in an *Independent* article titled, 'I was asked to stand for Remain in the Peterborough by-election – this is why I said no.'[4]

In the article, he says that he doesn't want to take votes from Labour and possibly aid Nigel Farage's Brexit Party, that he wasn't from Peterborough (he terms himself a 'Darlington-born Brummy who's never spent more than a day in that city') and that it would have been too much of a drain on his resources as he needed to focus on campaigning in the European elections. However, 'the truth is that our primary aim at that time had been, for two years, to convince Jeremy Corbyn to switch positions on Brexit,' Oluwole tells me, and 'if I'm campaigning in a by-election seat against Labour, that will make them see us like the enemy. And so we chose, well, it was decided collectively that the carrot approach was better than the stick approach.' Reporting in *The i* newspaper at the time suggested that he had been 'put under pressure from senior Labour figures', including some involved with the People's Vote campaign, to stand down.[5] The by-election was ultimately narrowly won by Labour's Lisa Forbes, with a majority of 683 votes; she would lose the seat just months later to Conservative Paul Bristow.

'I often wonder whether that was the right decision' not to stand, Oluwole tells me. 'If I had my time again, sure, I'd change a bunch of things; maybe that would be one of them.' But

> at the time, it felt like if I'm being told that this would be a major blow to the efforts to get the leader of the left to actually oppose Brexit and I choose to put my ability to enter Parliament above it, it felt like it might be self-indulgent, and I couldn't live with myself.

CHAPTER 15

IMPLOSION

Patrick Heneghan had had a long career in the Labour Party, rising to hold the post of director of elections between 2011 and 2017. After the change at the top in 2015, however, he found his politics – distinctly moderate – were not in line with the Corbyn leadership's. He was among the party staff named in a leaked report which alleged that, in a 'hyper-factional' environment, resources had been quietly diverted to preferred, non-Corbynite candidates at the 2017 election.[1] Heneghan himself has firmly denied this. 'The stab-in-the-back myth is their deflection from reality,' he said in 2020, terming the narrative a 'fantasy'. But clearly things were not harmonious between himself and the then leadership of the party, and he moved on from his role at Labour shortly after the 2017 election.

By late 2018 he was working for the People's Vote campaign, having been brought on at first as a consultant by Andrew Adonis. Tom Baldwin reports that Roland Rudd initially opposed this move 'because, he said, we're becoming too Labour', while Baldwin and McGrory initially supported it. Heneghan was, the communications director said, 'hugely expensive' to retain. It was clear what they wanted Heneghan for. In addition to his political alignment, the organisation run by two former spinners needed someone with an organising and data background at a high level. Who better than the man who'd been running Labour's elections? However, despite this, in the initial period, as one staffer remembered, Heneghan's actual duties were unclear. He was just 'kind of around. There were lots of people who were kind of around.'

In early 2019, in a move then supported by Baldwin and McGrory, it was proposed that Heneghan be installed as chief executive of the European Movement – an organisation that he knew little about and had little experience with, which was at the time chaired by former Tory Health Secretary Stephen Dorrell, who had OK'd the position. The move to, as Tom Brufatto put it, 'impose' Heneghan at the organisation was successful.

Mike Galsworthy – who is, it is worth noting, the current chair of the European Movement – was very unhappy with this development. 'I got on well with Patrick Heneghan,' he says, 'but I saw this as clearly a move to take this half of the People's Vote campaign and put it under the control of [the other] half.' It was, he thought, an attempt to bring the grassroots – Britain for Europe and its attendant groups were, after all, aligned with the European Movement – in line with the demands of the operation in Millbank headed by Baldwin and McGrory.

Heneghan being put in was, in Galsworthy's view,

> the moment that broke the People's Vote campaign utterly. Whoever concocted this plot was the person who broke the People's Vote campaign. Essentially, what happened was that, without any prior notice to anyone I knew, at a late-night regular meeting of the European Movement council, Patrick Heneghan was presented, by Dorrell to those few present, a bit was said about him, then they were asked to vote him in as their CEO while he was sat there in the room looking at them.

He continued:

> To say this was an unprofessional and aggressive move is an understatement. The council had had no forewarning and no ability to research and discuss. Not all of them were at the meeting. Tom Brufatto, who was effectively leading European Movement operations, was not consulted, despite being the person who was bolting on his own organisation, Britain for Europe, to the European Movement.

The European Movement had the longest pedigree of any organisation within the People's Vote campaign (it was the only one that was more than five years old) and was a meaningful hub of grassroots activism – probably, by 2019, the main hub, following its merger with Britain for Europe. However, people at Millbank doubted that this hub was being used as best it could have been. As Amanda Chetwynd-Cowieson of For our Future's Sake put it, the European Movement 'were good at turning people out for the big marches' and for other 'key visual moments'. But that being said, she

> would have expected that [the] European Movement could have found ways to grow their base as well. I'm sure they can reel off stats about how much their mailing list grew or whatever, but it actually didn't feel like they, as a movement, grew much over the course of the campaign.

This perception of resources being left on the table and, worse still, in the hands of grassroots activists viewed as more likely to don a bEUret than make a moderated appeal to soft Tories, prompted the move to install Heneghan.

'In one coup – and it was a coup – the uneasy truce and balance of the Open Britain/Joint Media Unit cluster and the European Movement/grassroots cluster was broken,' says Mike Galsworthy.

> The latter was forced to be subordinate to the former and there was no consultation on it. The naivety about ramifications was immense, as the grassroots were not local branches of a political party but legally independent entities increasingly pulling away from 'PVHQ' [People's Vote headquarters]. Tom [Brufatto] then had to disengage Britain for Europe from the European Movement, as that organisation would not accept the new arrangement.

By that point, Galsworthy says, he 'simply did not trust the People's Vote leadership at all'. Brufatto felt similarly.

'They could certainly run their own cult-like team in Millbank Tower – but they were so inept at wider diplomacy that they had zero chance of supporting any society-wide endeavour,' Galsworthy reckoned.

> At this point I thought the People's Vote campaign was screwed. I didn't want the People's Vote to break or for there to be any publicity around the fracture, but I simply made the calculation that whatever happened here, the local and independent groups all over the country needed the financing and support to be able to campaign in their areas on their own terms. That's what I set about doing. Get them funding, get them support, get their voices heard on their own terms. That's why Tom and I set up March for Change and ran a rally with it.

This group and this rally would prove to be another key moment in the break-up of the People's Vote campaign. If Galsworthy dated the collapse to Heneghan being put in at the European Movement, Baldwin dated it to the splinter over the march. Galsworthy and Brufatto's rally took place in July 2019, during the Conservative leadership race, and featured – as was popular at the time, following the Donald Trump baby balloon that had flown the year before – a small blimp shaped like Boris Johnson, wearing a T-shirt emblazoned with a bus that read '£350 million' and a pair of blue pants with red hearts.

While all the anti-Brexit marches tended to feature some anti-Johnson sentiment, this march was explicitly designed and reported on as a 'no to Boris' event.[2] Speakers included Oluwole and Billy Bragg. A BBC report shows a sea of European flags and a picture of Madeleina Kay wearing a crown and holding a sign that says 'Queen of European Hearts' and a blue guitar with a circle of yellow stars painted on it.

The event was ill looked on from Millbank, but less so – or so was the general perception – from Roland Rudd's offices on The Strand. The 'catalyst for break-up', Tom Baldwin explained,

> was when the Rudd faction announced another march without consulting the campaign leadership. We said it would be a disaster at that point, when we'd get lower numbers and, even worse, if it was explicitly to oppose Brexit. This was actually strategically moronic in terms of trying to sway Tory MPs with large Leave-voting constituents to back us and so we refused to back the march. Roland Rudd put the squeeze on us to back it via email lists and we refused. Rudd then told me, 'Well, I'm afraid things will become very difficult for you then.' And then the die, I guess, was cast.

Looking at the press coverage of the march, it's easy to understand why it caused frustration. While the write-up in Al Jazeera doesn't explicitly state that the march is part of the People's Vote campaign, a reader unfamiliar with the internal dynamics would very much assume that it was officially sanctioned by the broader campaign (it wasn't). Al Jazeera reported that 'as the march set off from Park Lane to chants of "Revoke, Remain; Brexit is a shame," a 2.7-metre "puppet master" Nigel Farage on stilts emerged, pulling the strings on two papier-mâché figures of Johnson and [Jeremy] Hunt'.[3] These puppets were courtesy of Best for Britain; as one Best for Britain staffer remembers, 'Those puppets we actually bought from Poland' and they had to have 'their own seats on the plane' on the way from Poland to the UK.

None of this was considered helpful. 'Having got, you know, 90 per cent of the PLP, we needed to start getting Conservative MPs on board,' Tom Baldwin reasoned. 'That was our strategic priority. Doing a "March for Europe" with a gigantic inflatable Boris Johnson – what was the purpose of that other than self-indulgence?' It would, to his view, 'reinforce everyone's prejudices against the movement'. One staffer said the overall perspective within the campaign on Galsworthy's effort was 'quite derisive'; another said, of Brufatto and Galsworthy, 'I think they would see themselves as bigger players than they were.'

A report in *The Observer* from 3 August 2019 – two weeks after the anti-Boris march – gives a clearer idea of what the campaign under McGrory and Baldwin would have preferred to focus on, detailing plans being put in place for a large-scale tactical voting campaign to back anti-Brexit candidates at a looming general election. This was in addition to ongoing lobbying work to sway soft Tory MPs. Earlier in the cycle, various staffers remember spending time in Eddisbury, drumming up local support for the campaign with the aim of swaying the then Tory MP for the area, Antoinette Sandbach. As one staffer put it, 'The thing about the People's Vote campaign was … the numbers were really in Parliament. It was about getting parliamentary support.' Alastair Campbell was of a similar view, asserting to UK in a Changing Europe that 'it was only winnable if you could win it in Parliament'.[4] The marches had some effect on moving public opinion and making the campaign look weighty to MPs, but they were ultimately ancillary to making the parliamentary maths add up in favour of a new vote. A march that was so directly geared towards criticism of the then leader of the Conservative Party was viewed by some as stepping from ancillary to genuinely unhelpful.

'There were a lot of people who really genuinely believed, and I'm trying not to sound too disparaging, but who really genuinely believed that, like, one more march' would get the referendum over the line, one People's Vote staffer told me.

> For the base, that's what they wanted. I mean, these people from, you know, branch chairman of European Movement Southwest or whatever … they weren't wholly wrong about wanting to be able to inspire their swelling membership, but it was very distracting and very unhelpful in lots of ways.

To get the result, they say, 'you had to sway the Labour leadership and you had to persuade, I can't remember what the numbers were, but like thirty Tory MPs and that was the only path through – vanishing, unlikely path as it was'. For those critical of the March for Europe, what the grassroots wanted was not good – was in fact actively detrimental – to the delicate cause of securing a new vote. When, as one staffer involved told me, you are 'focused in large part on the One Nation Tories', making the leader of the Tory Party a bogeyman (or bogeyblimp) was not, to their view, wise.

Galsworthy speaks highly of the march:

> It achieved our core objectives – all grassroots voices on stage, no politicians. Also the message 'No to Boris, Yes to Europe' just before Johnson was appointed hit the BBC, *Daily Mail*, *Guardian*, *Independent* and translated beautifully into all the European languages for their press. It even hit the press in New Zealand! We flew a big blimp of Boris Johnson and packed Parliament Square. It was a great day – and the grassroots came away feeling empowered and that they were being heard on their own terms and in an overtly pro-European way.

Baldwin, meanwhile, doesn't: 'Their march was a flop. They got 20,000 people.'

Heneghan, having been brought in by them and sharing their political background, was initially seen as and assumed to be a down-the-line ally of Baldwin, McGrory, Mandelson and Campbell. As befits this positioning, Baldwin remembers, Heneghan had 'helped us oppose the March for Europe thing'. However, shortly after this, again per Baldwin, he was 'suddenly off having secret meetings with Roland'. As Richard Brooks remembers, 'It became clear that Patrick was, I guess to a certain extent, a voice for [Roland],' an alliance which 'certainly felt like it was built on a bit of a mutual distrust and dislike of Tom and James'.

It looked like Heneghan had switched sides – and by this point, in the summer of 2019, there were very much sides. Previously, Rudd had been hands off. As Mike Galsworthy put it, 'He was often AWOL. He didn't know the staff below senior level. Lovely guy, charming manner, with never any ill will to anyone but oftentimes just absent and negligent on the engagement front.' The staff of the campaign tended to have a harsher view: when he did have to interact with them, one staffer said, he viewed them as 'NPCs' (non-player characters) and 'irrelevant people'.

If McGrory and Baldwin hadn't warmed to Hugo Dixon, Rudd's right-hand man who'd allegedly been made in a lab to annoy Alastair Campbell, they hadn't warmed to Rudd either. One incident Mance highlights was a media appearance Rudd did down the phone from the Davos summit, which also came up in several interviews I conducted. Baldwin was, he said, trying to run a professional campaign with the likes of McGrory and Rachel Kinnock,

> and then you had other people who saw it as sort of a vanity badge. It wasn't helpful having Roland Rudd introduced on the *Today* programme as 'the chair of the People's Vote campaign live from Davos' when we were trying to show we weren't part of a remote elite and no one had appointed him as chair of the campaign in the first place.

I asked Richard Brooks to summarise the tensions and the make-up of the two groups. He told me that it

> became increasingly clear over 2019 that there was a political, strategic tension between, I think, particularly Tom, but Tom and James's view. Which [was], now we just get parliamentary [support for] a People's Vote and that means you need to have people who are not naturally inclined to back a People's Vote, which means that the campaign needs to speak in a particular way, speak to certain audiences etc., versus the Rudd view.

Of Rudd's view, Brooks says, 'To be honest, I still sometimes struggle to rationalise it' but characterises it as being motivated by 'slight self-interest, probably a bit of money, probably a bit of having the data we need to keep our activists' and the need 'to keep our activists happy'. The outcome reasoned from this, Brooks says, is the conclusion that 'holistically, we need to be in a revoke space [with] lots of marches'.

Another staffer highlighted the difference in approach:

> It was the people who were in the JMU and with the youth groups that kind of got that a bit and wanted to keep it about the vote. The principle of the vote, however you voted, whether you were Leave or whether you were Remain, keep it focused on that. And the people who wanted it to be the Remain campaign, assuming we'd get a vote and this would then become the Remain body. And my view is that Roland was firmly in that latter camp.

Amanda Chetwynd-Cowieson of FFS was of a similar view, noting that Rudd increasingly moved into alliance with the grassroots of the campaign, who were less interested in the 'choice' and democracy angle of the second referendum ask, but wasn't quite willing to put it all down to a question of ideology: 'I wouldn't put Roland Rudd automatically in that bracket, because Roland Rudd's number-one interest in life is Roland Rudd.'

The fact that Heneghan had come out of the Labour right and been manoeuvred into place by a certain part of the campaign probably, in one staffer's estimation, 'entrenched the sense of treachery' when he went in with Rudd. The view arose among some that Rudd and Dixon (aided by Heneghan) were trying to undermine McGrory and Baldwin's good work out of little more than narcissism and a desire for control – or, if you took a different view, that Rudd, Dixon and Heneghan were trying to right the imbalance of power that the organisation's imperfect governance had created by prudently seeking to rein in an out-of-control Baldwin and McGrory. In some people's views, any attempt at reasoning out the motivations was misguided, as what all this ultimately came down to was a titanic clash of egos.

'What we didn't know was that … there was quite a lot of stuff we thought was being done on the ground which actually wasn't being done,' said Tom Baldwin. A more junior staffer described Heneghan as 'terrible' to work with; another remembered him being 'lairy' on a staff night out. Corbyn spinner James Schneider also questioned his competence, alleging that

Heneghan approached him with a job offer. 'I knew that also their operation was not terribly competent because, I mean, I was approached by Patrick Heneghan to be the director of comms for the second referendum campaign. And, I mean, this is how, like, not smart they were.' Schneider says he found this baffling, although it's not clear that he holds Heneghan in greater contempt than he does anyone else involved in the People's Vote campaign. Heneghan denies having made this approach.

If the tension had been building for a time, the spark that set it off, according to Baldwin, was a report commissioned into the governance of the campaign. Again, while no one disputes the facts of the report, which said the campaign needed serious structural reform, there was a diametric difference in opinion on how the response to this should be handled by the two sides. The report was dubbed 'Project Marshall'. It was penned by Henry Stannard and designed with a very forward-looking motivation: to iron out governance issues and hopefully enable the People's Vote campaign to transform seamlessly into the designated campaign to Remain should the referendum they all wanted actually come about. A second report was titled 'Project Root' and was designed to look into the mistakes of Britain Stronger in Europe, to make sure they weren't repeated.[5] Baldwin says that Rudd used Project Marshall as a 'gotcha' to get rid of him and James McGrory, pinning its broader commentary about how the campaign needed to change on them.

'It became quite clear that Roland was preparing a coup

against the leadership of the campaign,' says Tom Baldwin, 'because his bag man was marching into the office demanding James sign legal documentation handing over control of the data and the bank accounts to Roland Rudd directly.' Baldwin says they tried to put it off:

> James had delayed signing until basically faced [with] the subpoena, like he was gonna have to go to court. We had been trying to create a new governance for the campaign, basically setting up the kind of structure we needed if there was a referendum, because there's no way you could fight and win with nine different organisations all thinking they were in complete control. You need to have professional people. They need to have political leadership.

One development which very much did not help matters in terms of trust came in August 2019, when an email thread of discussion between anti-Rudd board members and other figures in the campaign was accidentally forwarded to the whole of the board by Stephen Dorrell (who profusely apologised for having circulated, among other things, some 'disobliging personal remarks'). The revealing thread showed that Rudd's opponents wanted to get rid of or work around him and were unhappy with his and Dixon's support for the Galsworthy–Brufatto splinter march. Perhaps most notably, it showed that a 'public battle' for control was considered inevitable; this was, of course, not wrong.

Things came to a head on the night of Sunday 27 October

2019, just a week after the last big march had pulled in 700,000 people, when Rudd announced in an email to all staff that Baldwin and McGrory had been fired and that Patrick Heneghan would be taking over as CEO. A general election was looming, as everyone knew (it would be called days later, on the 31st). Detailing his reasoning to Henry Mance, Rudd said, 'We needed to do more to focus on digital and data operations, which had been hugely neglected. Frankly, it was not 1997 any more.' Three board members who didn't side with Rudd were, per Mance, 'forced out'.[6]

The three, Peter Mandelson, Joe Carberry – who had initially been McGrory's co-director – and Will Straw, who had led the Britain Stronger in Europe campaign, wrote a joint and incredibly condemnatory letter to Rudd. They wrote that he had 'contributed little to the strategy of Open Britain, preferring to use board meetings to focus on structures and corporate manoeuvres' and alleged that the board chair had 'done Boris Johnson's work for him. He could not have hoped for a more compliant advocate on the Remain side and owes you a debt of gratitude. Whereas the People's Vote campaign has been a movement of millions, for you it has been simply a vehicle for your ego.' Interestingly, they also allege that Rudd had previously said he would stand aside for a female chair but had not done so.

Richard Brooks remembers getting the email firing Baldwin and McGrory. 'I remember feeling quite physically sick,' he says. 'At that time, I smoked. So, I went outside, smoked a cigarette and then I called Amanda and I think I called Jason [his For our Future's Sake co-founders] before trying to reach Tom and James.' He was not the only one: their phones were engaged.

Reporting on tensions by Alex Wickham and others had shed some light on the situation for the outside world, but once the email went out a new level of public scrutiny descended. The next morning, both Rudd and Baldwin appeared on the *Today* programme. Baldwin accused Rudd of putting a 'wrecking ball' through the campaign. 'He's making the mistake that a lot of businessmen do when they dabble in politics, which is to think that because they have a certain title on the board, that they then own the campaign,' said Baldwin, speaking with calm and well-chewed contempt for Rudd. A more flustered Rudd initially insisted that there was no problem and said that Baldwin 'has an opportunity for a different type of role' but that 'we need to have a proper, civilised chat' about the situation, alluding to unhappiness over overly party-political stances.

Rudd had scheduled an emergency meeting at 9 a.m., so the unhappy staff – who had quickly organised themselves into a WhatsApp group called 'OMG', which I am told is still going – met at 8 a.m. 'We all gathered in the Our Future, Our Choice office. They had, I think, the smallest office out of everyone, so everyone's kind of sat on the floor,' Bashir Ibrahim remembers. 'I believe that Tom and James had to be brought in because their cards were immediately deactivated.'

It would, Ibrahim says, 'be very dishonest to say' that there was any kind of 'coherent' plan or strategy at the meeting, because 'we were in shock. We needed a space to be like, WTF. What the hell is going on?' He adds that they were also attempting to work out 'how we can handle this meeting' coming up with Rudd. He thinks 'the primary purpose of that was to make sure that we weren't gonna accept what happened', and to make it clear that 'we stood firmly with James and Tom'.

'James was like, don't get angry,' expressing, Ibrahim said, the view that 'Roland needs to, at a minimum, come and address you guys, because it was really discourteous just to send an email on a Sunday' changing so much about the campaign on which they'd worked so hard with no consultation. One of the options discussed was a staff walkout.

'I think James sort of came into his own a bit as a leader' in the aftermath of the Rudd email, Richard Brooks said.

> The thing that I think impressed lots of people, certainly convinced lots of people, was it didn't feel like [you have to do this] my way or you're with me or with Rudd. He didn't make people choose. He said, this is the situation, and you guys are gonna have to make a choice. I'm not going to force you because there will be consequences, but this is what I'm planning on doing.

At the end of it, knowing that in all likelihood they would be walking out after their meeting with Rudd that morning, they realised a final thing. It was Bashir Ibrahim's birthday. They sang their song one last time before going out to talk to Rudd. Ibrahim remembers it as emotional: 'It was the final time we were all properly together in Millbank.'

The staff went to the Open Britain offices. As Ibrahim remembers, they were 'waiting in this room and no one's come to come and speak to us'. On Twitter, 'lots of colour from journalists' was appearing – 'some of it, obviously, was being briefed by us'. Ibrahim says they eventually realised that Rudd was downstairs but wouldn't speak to the group while McGrory and Baldwin were there (their key cards, remember, had been deactivated). Rudd went on Sky News instead of attending and sent up Heneghan to talk to them. He walked in to 'pin-drop silence' and offered them what Ibrahim described as 'weaselly words'.

The staff walked out. Press coverage continued, with an article appearing in *The Guardian* just after noon that day informing the world that 'dozens of staff at People's Vote have staged a walkout in protest at moves by the PR guru Roland Rudd to force two leading figures out of the organisation, plunging the campaign for a second referendum further into chaos'.[7]

'To this day,' says Alastair Campbell,

> I do not understand why Roland Rudd did what he did, but he basically dropped a hand-grenade into the whole thing, and got rid of James McGrory and Tom Baldwin, who are both flawed, but we like flawed people. Campaigns need people who do not just fit a very ordinary mould. They were both incredibly energetic, incredibly hard-working and they were doing good stuff.[8]

Another staff meeting was called for the next day, Tuesday, and held in a room at the nearby Hilton Hotel. Brooks describes this meeting as 'the maddest ninety minutes of my professional life'. The chaos began before the meeting even started, as two bouncers had been stationed at the door, seemingly for the sole purpose of keeping Baldwin and McGrory out. The pair's back and forth with the security men was civil but all caught on camera by the Guido Fawkes website, whose reporter did a piece to camera from the throng of staffers at the door of the meeting room. FFS staffer Cathleen Clarke is filming in shot, while just past the bouncers Amanda Chetwynd-Cowieson can be seen pacing. 'It's a pretty unpleasant experience for young members of staff to see two pretty serious-looking geezers stopping colleagues coming into a meeting,' says McGrory. 'I appreciate you've got a job to do,' says Baldwin after establishing that it's only him and McGrory who are to be turned away.[9]

Inside the meeting room, things did not improve. The meeting was a mess. Rudd had, it was clear, lost all legitimacy in the eyes of the staff, who accused him of consulting no one before taking action to remove McGrory and Baldwin and insert Heneghan. Allegations of inappropriate conduct towards female staff members were levelled against Patrick Heneghan, which he denied and was later cleared of following an investigation into his conduct by a legal firm. These allegations had also been shared via email the night before, following Rudd's email, with staff members arguing that Rudd had not taken that into consideration when he had made the decision to appoint Heneghan as CEO. There were calls for Heneghan to be suspended and many, many calls for Rudd to resign. People spoke about feeling worried in their jobs. Others spoke in defence of McGrory and, when told that Rudd felt the organisation needed a new CEO, asked why Baldwin had also been removed. Rudd's support for Galsworthy's breakaway March for Europe was again a subject of contention (Rudd denied supporting it).

At one point, a straw poll of hands was taken on the question of whether the room had confidence in Rudd as chair of the People's Vote campaign. The result was 40–3 against. Rudd said he would do all he could to win back their support. This was met with derision.

Charlie Atkins remembers one exchange with Rudd at the meeting when the board chair 'was trying to do this whole thing of like, we've been through a lot together. And someone was like, "No, we haven't. What's my name?" And then he was just like, well, I don't know your name.' Those who were opposed to Baldwin and McGrory viewed their relationship with the staff as inorganic and insincere, developed as a part of a broader ploy. The walkout by staff, said one person I spoke to who was of this view, 'was months in the making' and had been planned by McGrory as part of his war with Rudd. But say what you will about Tom Baldwin and James McGrory: they knew everyone's names.

The affair at the Hilton, it is fair to say, went very badly and did so very publicly. The staff walked out, again, and set up camp at The Grosvenor pub. As Luke Myer remembered, there was 'a strange wartime feel' to the set-up in the staffers' local. He took some notes about it at the time, recording

> small teams setting up camp on makeshift workspaces. The walls of the pub are covered with antique pistols and model naval ships. There's a group by the ladies toilets contacting key allies from MPs to public figures, another wrangling with legal issues from the pool table, a third group commandeering some sticky booths to contact the press. The landlord was very gracious and happy to have so many captive customers.

Brooks describes the choice to walk out as 'really hard'. One staffer described it as

> a really painful split, because there's some people who genuinely thought, 'Look, I hate what's going on, but I have to try and win this thing and so I'm just going to try and keep doing my job.' And then those of us on the other side who walked … we also wanted to win the thing, but we just couldn't see how it was possible with Roland's approach. They just didn't understand media. They didn't understand politics at all. So, yeah, it was very messy.

The Grosvenor was the end of the line for the People's Vote campaign. In the outside world, its organisations met various fates. For our Future's Sake managed to extricate itself and ran tactical voting operations in the 2019 election. Several members of Our Future Our Choice – including Ed Shackle and Lara Spirit – had already departed the scene by the time of the breakdown and were running a youth voter registration drive called Vote For Your Future, but there was a general perception, Richard Brooks says, that OFOC had sided with Rudd or, at least, did not decisively side with Baldwin and McGrory. The old rivalries between the two organisations couldn't quite be dispelled. 'I lost a lot of respect, in particular for Will and Femi, at the end,' says Brooks. Scientists for EU is still going and still posting. But the umbrella campaign fell apart hard and could not be put back together again.

Of course, it was not a coincidence that the People's Vote campaign died when it did; it blew up due to conflicts between individuals, but it also just ran out of political road. By the time everyone was yelling at each other in the Hilton, an election was inevitable and the game was up. One staffer said they reckoned things were over

> when Boris went to meet Varadkar and came back with a new deal. It really took the air out the balloon, because we'd spent so much time saying how bad no deal was. But this is a deal. A deal was better than either of these chaotic things [no deal or a new referendum] and people were just like, fucking tired of it.

The whole thing was, says Baldwin, 'ridiculously messy'. He would, he says, have acted differently with the benefit of hindsight, but at the time, emotions were running very high.

> We fought like tigers, partly because that's what we'd been doing for the previous two years and we were campaigners. By October 2019, I should have probably said, just walk away. But we fought on, partly because we felt an obligation to the staff. They were brilliant and had stood up for us. Some of them were on London living wage. These weren't rich people. And you had a bunch of multi-millionaires playing fucking games.

Luke Myer strikes a similar note:

> It's frustrating, I think, because the whole mess started with Cameron, you know, very posh guy, very rich guy, creating this mess and then walking away. And then it ended with a very posh, very rich guy creating a mess and then ultimately resigning and walking away. I mean, this campaign had hundreds of thousands of emails, had a massive war chest. It could have been one of the most powerful tools in any election.

The now-MP continued: 'It's like he was playing at politics, you know – just this idea that you can be a hugely wealthy guy and just, carry out a boardroom takeover of a massive campaign that's been built by grassroots campaigners and it'll somehow keep working.'

'Anybody involved in that dispute, as a broad brush,' says Femi Oluwole,

> I will never forgive, because those of us who gave up everything

> in our lives – I left all of my friends in Vienna, my job in Vienna, the woman I was seeing in Vienna, my apartment in Vienna, left Austria to come back to the UK and take death threats for two years because I did not give a shit about myself. I only cared about the cause or preventing all the damage Brexit would do.

'I know that there was a #MeToo issue happening at the same time,' he says, in reference to the allegations against Heneghan, 'so anybody who took issue with it on that basis I support,' but 'in general I take a "pox on both of your houses" approach'.

Ultimately, you can choose to take the view that Rudd, and with him Dixon, Heneghan and Galsworthy and a host of others, were in the wrong, or you can choose to lay the blame at the feet of McGrory, Baldwin, Campbell and the staff who walked out (and a host of others). Tim Shipman's account of the affair, in his book *Out*, ends up in what I'd assess as an anti-Rudd position: 'Nearly everyone who worked on the campaign gave the lion's share of the credit for its successes to McGrory and Baldwin – exasperating for Rudd, whose ego was visible from space.'[10] This is in line with the widely accepted narrative you will hear in Westminster. This narrative, I think, does not fully take into account the relationships and perspectives of the grassroots (which I have tried to reflect in this work), who had a dubious view of McGrory and Baldwin. Nonetheless, it seems to me broadly fair and, in as much as such interpersonally contested things can be understood to be accurate, accurate.

However, to some people – and this also strikes me as neither unfair nor inaccurate – it was everyone's fault: an inevitable, tectonic clash of egos. 'I do remember someone tweeting,' one staffer remembers, saying, 'Oh, you're saying that getting a collection of the most toxic people in British politics together in one building didn't work out?' To which the staffer's view is, 'No shit. Roland Rudd and Alastair Campbell got into a dick-measuring contest and that ended badly.' In their view, badly was pretty much the only way it ever could have ended. It takes two to tango and even more to create an atmosphere that was, to Naomi Smith's view, 'toxic,' where 'knives were out left, right and centre.' As Geeta Sidhu-Robb – appointed to the Open Britain board by Rudd, a former lawyer turned founder of Nosh Detox, which sells pricey juice cleanses – memorably told Henry Mance, 'I've done oil deals in Russia, and I've never seen anything like it.'[11]

To the view of Laura Parker, an unwillingness to let go of ego and one's own place in the spotlight was one of the things that blighted the campaign. For a successful re-run, she says, you would 'need a total reconfiguration of the people in charge, i.e. most of the people in charge needed to not be in charge. Or they needed to bring their expertise, which some of them undoubtedly had' and stay out of the spotlight.

> If you had Alastair Campbell in the background giving comms advice, it will probably be helpful, but don't make him the spokesperson. Roland Rudd, financing – helpful. Don't have him on Radio 4 down the line from Davos, talking about the Remain campaign. Jolyon Maugham giving legal advice, absolutely. Would any of these people be the right people to front it up? No.

There was not, ultimately, a People's Vote. But the campaign was arguably a surprisingly successful flop. 'Much as it was an absolute and complete failure,' one staffer reflects, it was

> genuinely impressive that they managed to get as far as they did, to get it as close to the idea it might be imaginable as they did. Because I think in the end, it's fucking mad – you can't say to a country two years after they've just had this once-in-a-lifetime thing and all voted on something, 'Well, actually, we think you should do it again.' Like, that is a mad proposition. And the fact that they were able to message it into a form of respectability, I think, is a big comms achievement.

PART V

NEW CENTRIST PARTIES

CHAPTER 16

CHANGE UK

The upheavals and public unhappiness over Brexit brought about much talk of, if you will recall, a GNU – a government of national unity – including, per one suggestion by Caroline Lucas, a GNU composed entirely of women. *The Guardian* wrote it up as 'an extraordinary proposal that will be viewed with scepticism by rival parties'.[1] The period inculcated in many politicians and wannabe politicians the idea that now was the time to gamble, that the underlying structures of British politics could break apart and that new parties could thrive. The entire political settlement of this period was founded on risk and long shot, after all – that of calling the referendum and of Leave winning against the odds – so, as some thought, why not me? To paraphrase Lenin, many people, notably Chuka Umunna, felt that power was lying in the streets and thought they could be the ones to pick it up. Invariably, they couldn't, but along the way they did establish a great many new centrist parties, littering the internet with dried-up Twitter accounts and dead websites, desiccated woodlice in the attic of our polity.

The loudest calls for a new party were coming from inside the Labour Party. Most Labour MPs were not happy when Jeremy Corbyn became party leader and were even less so when Britain voted to leave the EU. They attempted to get rid of him in the summer of 2016; they failed. Discontent swirled and took the form of threats and suggestions that a new party might break away. One such discontented Labour MP was Mike Gapes, who had represented Ilford South since 1992. It was a new pose for him. 'My whole time in Parliament, I'd been regarded pretty much as a loyalist,' he explains. He'd rarely rebelled against the party whip.

Gapes had been a firm Corbyn critic and an early supporter of the second referendum – despite having himself voted to leave in the 1975 referendum – and describes the whole post-2017 election period as 'intensive, non-stop, every day for about two years. It was just consuming all our energies.' While Starmer gave Gapes a more favourable impression over time, Gapes 'wasn't convinced' the shadow Brexit Secretary was a sincere supporter of a new vote. He found Corbyn himself to be a 'strange mixture of non-engaged or hostile' on the topic. In early 2018, his discontent being generally known, he was approached by others wishing to discuss 'where we were going, given the terrible state the Labour Party was in.'

By the middle of 2018, he says,

> there were three real groups in the PLP who were critical of Corbyn. There were the people who wanted to keep their heads down and do nothing. There were the people who were

> really concerned ... there was an informal ... WhatsApp group called the Birthday Club, which brought together loads of members of the PLP. [It] had probably eighty to one hundred people. And then there was a third group of people who were really coming to the view that we can't go on like this.

It was not solely Brexit that animated this last group – concerns over antisemitism, a perception of a changed culture in the party and Corbyn's handling of the Skripal poisonings also featured in their thinking – but it was a key element. Gapes describes himself, by the end of 2018, as 'anguished' about the state of the party. In the autumn of that year, he was 'asked to join a group who were seriously considering what to do, whether to, when or if or how, to leave'. This group, the final circle of the discontented, would indeed break away from the party in February 2019, as first The Independent Group (TIG), then The Independent Group for Change, then Change UK. It initially constituted of Gapes and his fellow Labour MPs Gavin Shuker, Ann Coffey, Luciana Berger, Angela Smith, Chris Leslie and Chuka Umunna. They would later be joined by the Labour MP Joan Ryan and the Conservative MPs Anna Soubry, Heidi Allen and Sarah Wollaston. By the close of poll on 12 December 2019, all of them would have lost their seats.

In many ways, they fell at the first hurdle: the European Parliament elections, which took place just a few months after their launch. The party had been caught up in making sure its launch went well – which, broadly, it did – and then with fighting bad press that followed a media appearance by Angela

Smith where she infamously described people from ethnic minority backgrounds as having 'a funny tinge'. They were left to get ready for the May elections in some hurry. 'There was a mad dash to get a full slate in each region,' one Change UK staffer remembers. As they recall, the party

> got such weird applications. Honestly, they turned down one from Richard Dawkins to stand because they thought, no, he's actually too much of a wild card, and he's going to say something that pisses off every religion under the sun. We can't actually have Richard Dawkins. But they didn't really do due diligence on most of these people.

Another hitch came when the party registered with the Electoral Commission. They were told, the staffer recalls, that 'they weren't allowed to call themselves The Independent Group, because the word independent is reserved for independents, funnily enough'. They would be listed on the ballot paper as Change UK The Independent Group.

After this, the nascent party, according to the Change UK staffer,

> then had to pull a whole brand-new name and branding and everything out their arse, with no money whatsoever … I think they gave the logo design people for Change UK a week. And usually, if you've ever gone through this kind of thing with corporate clients, they will have six months to a year and actual money. And so it's no wonder that the logo was bad. It's

> no wonder that the name was bad, because they just had to put something on the form.

The logo was initially rejected by the Electoral Commission for featuring '#change', as links to online content are not permitted. Another logo – a series of black and white stripes that brings to mind Cornish nationalism and possibly also ska music, but does not particularly trigger thoughts of moderated professional pro-Europeanism – was widely panned. The branding was the subject of an article in *WIRED* magazine, which thought 'the four solid black bars feel quite brutal, like something has been crossed out, blocked or obscured'.[2] The article, by a creative director, argued that the branding problems would be off-putting to voters, who 'will read this sense of confusion, uncertainty and naivety as a reflection of what's going on internally within the party'.

'We thought we could get a seat in London' at the European elections, Mike Gapes recalls, but they fell significantly short. 'We had no infrastructure and no members, so it was all completely difficult.' The Liberal Democrats turning in an improved performance at that year's local elections didn't help them either.

'If you were planning to establish a political party,' Gapes reflects, 'you should probably establish it a year to two before any elections. You probably need to have a development of a policy platform and so on. Over a period of months, you should have established your membership.' Change UK had none of this, says Gapes: 'I described it as a series of unfortunate events. I used to read that book to my daughter years ago, and it really was one thing that went wrong after another.' They won precisely no seats at the European elections; after that, the MPs began to splinter and scatter, with Berger and Umunna joining the Liberal Democrats.

If there had been fears within the Labour Party about defections, for many, the haphazard actuality of the thing itself put them to bed. 'Once I saw Change UK launch, or the Independent Group, or whatever they were called, I was pretty confident there wasn't going to be some mass outpouring of Labour MPs, because it was just shambolic,' said then Labour head of policy Andrew Fisher. 'Clearly, there was a lot of egos involved with very different politics, mainly personal politics. You couldn't see that vast swathes of Labour MPs were going to go, "I want to fall under the magnificent leadership of Chuka Umunna or Anna Soubry."'[3]

In discussions of the ill-fated party, Umunna was often depicted as a man whose ego outpaced events. In this telling, he wanted to be in charge and didn't think hard enough about what it was that he was in charge of or its long-term viability. Whether it was ego is a matter of perspective, but I think it's certainly fair to understand Change UK as impatient; if they had kept their powder dry, there's a good chance Umunna would be in the Cabinet as I write this. A staffer working for one of the breakaway MPs at the time took a more sympathetic view, arguing that 'people like Chuka Umunna and Anna Soubry were accused of being very cynical and duplicitous and plotting and all this kind of stuff, where actually, of their entire careers in Parliament, that was them at their most sincere'. The closer they got to breaking away – supporting a People's Vote, more and more openly criticising their respective parties – they were 'finding their principles in the way that they were constantly accused of not having any' and becoming ever 'more comfortable … in their own skin'.

Suspicions that it might incubate a new party stuck to the People's Vote campaign and not without justification: 'There were wannabe McKinsey slide decks going round about the new parties all these people were gonna do… like San Francisco post-Facebook going big and everyone decided that they were going to build a social network,' one staffer remembered. It was an organisation packed full of people who'd been big under New Labour, and the single biggest guy under New Labour – Tony Blair himself – was reported to be actively interested in the prospect of a breakaway. Patrick Maguire and Gabriel Pogrund wrote that Blair came to the view that Labour was 'too weak to win, but too strong to die', while 'Jonathan Powell, Blair's former chief of staff, went from boardroom to boardroom seeking converts among Labour donors'.[4] As Tom Brufatto remembers, 'the stuff about the new parties was constantly swirling around. At times it felt like there was talk of a different new party every day of the week.'

The idea of a new, more moderate, pro-European party was not a novel one in British politics, nor indeed a novel one to many of the people involved in the campaign for a new referendum. If part of the suspicion around the People's Vote campaign's possible role in a new party was down to the wandering eyes of Blair and some around him, another layer of suspicion was due, I think in part, to the histories of some of those involved. Hugo Dixon and Roland Rudd had, after all, both started off their working lives with the SDP, a new, more moderate, pro-European party that had split from Labour decades before. Andrew Adonis, another very active figure in the People's Vote campaign, has written about joining the SDP 'a few days after my eighteenth birthday in 1981' and subsequently was elected as an SDP councillor.[5]

To get a closer look at the parallels and prehistory, I spoke to Nick Garland, a historian of modern British politics, whose work explores the origins of the SDP. He says, 'If you think about the formation of the SDP, the two really defining breaches with Labour are first over Europe and secondly and more generally over the rise of the left.' The latter was particularly inflected with a 'real distaste for the culture of the hard left'. Looking then at the circumstances around the creation of the People's Vote and the Change UK breakaway, Garland adds, there are 'parallels to this combination'. These parallels are also drawn, unflatteringly, by Andrew Fisher, who disdained Umunna, Soubry et al. as 'not substantial enough politicians. They are not Shirley Williams and they're not the SDP, in essence.'[6]

The average person who joined the SDP, however, did not come from another party. As Garland explains, 'the average SDP member was not a member of any party before 1981 and did not see the party as a party of the left,' a type into which, he says, both Andrew Adonis and Danny Finkelstein's youthful stints in the SDP can be sorted. The appeal to these members was not an escape from Labour bruiserism but was often 'elevating ideas of moderation' and professionalism.

'There are a lot of very uncharitable cliches about the SDP as being claret-drinking – the references to claret are everywhere – and this idea that they had a certain decadent, bourgeois' affect, Garland explains. There was a characterisation of the party as one of 'doctors and various professional middle-class do-gooders who like to get involved in things'. While it can be overplayed, there's 'definitely some truth to that', he says. I would also find it hard not to draw a fairly direct comparison with the way anti-Brexit activists were spoken about. Both the SDP and the anti-Brexit movement, Garland thinks, can be understood as a 'movementism of the centre'. He also argues that Raphael Samuel's critique of the SDP as the 'democracy of the well placed' could reasonably also be applied to the movement against Brexit. Both were, he says, 'trying to appeal to people who expected to have their voices heard'. There is, of course, a lot of class politics going on here but also class of a certain era. Dixon and Rudd's biographies are, Garland says, 'not atypical of people who came into the SDP quite young and had very distinguished careers,' which is partly 'a testament to another time where people could sort of float between politics, journalism, bit of academia, bit of business' in a way that is no longer really possible.

However warranted the suspicions that the People's Vote might be a front – or even just a friend – to a new party, the new party actually breaking away was a weight off the mind of some within the campaign. The threat of a split from Labour had loomed over the People's Vote campaign for the first year of its existence. When Change UK finally happened, it was in many ways something of a relief, even if they immediately began to rub up against the campaign. As Tom Baldwin remembers:

> When TIG started, they did what Chuka had been trying to do for ages, which was create a mechanism for a vote in the House of Commons which would lever off lots of Labour MPs against Corbyn and then see whether they would withdraw and then create a big group. And so they tabled this amendment for immediate effect. We knew that would be strategically disastrous, because at most it would win support from maybe just 100-odd MPs and in doing so only demonstrate our weakness, rather than our strength.

This was not what Baldwin wanted. In his view, 'the only purpose it would serve would be to create a bigger pool from which the likes of Chuka could fish for more recruits. So, it served their purpose in creating a new party but didn't serve our purposes in winning a People's Vote.'

The campaign group responded to the amendment:

> We got a message through to Keir who said, from the despatch box, 'I've got a message here from the People's Vote campaign that they don't support this amendment.' There was some fury from Chuka and that lot who'd thought all along that we would hand over the whole campaign to them.

Given that that wasn't the case, Baldwin says, 'once we'd separated ourselves from the TIGs, things become much easier with the Labour leadership. McDonnell and people like that became quite open to us.'

'Chuka jumped early for no apparent advantage,' in Baldwin's reckoning. 'The Labour Party wasn't finished. That's been shown by Keir's victory at this last election.' He's also fairly clear when I ask whether there was any temptation to join forces with the splitters: 'We didn't go with Chuka because our purpose was to get a People's Vote, and we weren't interested in anything else.'

Change UK wasn't solely about Brexit, of course – Jeremy Corbyn being leader of the Labour Party was probably the more important underlying context for the initial split. Nonetheless, leaving the European Union provided them with a grander, more external cause, one that would bring in disaffected Tory MPs to what was originally a Labour Party splinter. What electoral prospects they hoped to have were bound up in their ability to capitalise on public anti-Brexit feeling. That this ability proved to be somewhere between limited and non-existent can't be taken wholesale as an indication of the electorate's interest in pro-Europeanism (from the bungled logo onwards, the party didn't manage to make itself seem like a viable prospect), but it does shed light on the limits and difficulties of mining these sentiments at the polls.

CHAPTER 17

... AND THE REST

Change UK was big news in British politics (for a bit). But there were many, many other, smaller attempts at new parties in this period, some of which stood candidates at elections and some of which were, in the real meaning of the word, simply delusions. If parallels with the SDP allow us to better understand Change UK, what these parties were usually aiming for (often explicitly) was the UKIP model: to be a small, irritant party, which will never win significant power but which moves the discourse on a key issue. After all, what was UKIP but the original pro-second referendum party?

Vying with Change UK for votes in the London region at the 2019 European elections was the UKEU Party, which stood four candidates in the capital. Its pitch, in the crowded field, was that it was the most Remain party out there, supportive of reversing Brexit (of course) but also of creating an EU defence force and joining the euro. It was led by lawyer Pierre Kirk and did, at least, have something of a strategy: targeting Europeans living in London who were eligible to vote in the EU elections. As Kirk told the *Evening Standard*, 'The wildcard vote in this election is that of the EU citizens, and we are quietly confident we will get the votes of this wildcard.'[1] Their pitch was, he said, being 'the only one that is completely pro-Europe – we are the most remain party. Fifty per cent of our candidates are born outside of the UK.' They did not win any seats. Kirk stood for the party at the Peterborough by-election – which, as you will recall, Femi Oluwole opted not to contest as an anti-Brexit candidate – and won twenty-five votes.

In October 2017 it was reported in the *Financial Times* that a man named Chris Coghlan, who had run as an independent anti-Brexit candidate in Battersea at the 2017 general election, was among those involved in setting up a new party. Titled 'Renew' (subtitle: 'new party, new hope'), they were supportive of a new referendum on Brexit and, according to the *Financial Times*, planned 'to offer voters a mix of environmentalism, modest tax rises to restore the public finances and "aggressive housebuilding"'.[2]

'The politicians from both major parties have failed us,' Coghlan told the *Financial Times*, explaining the space he thought existed for Renew. 'They've been hijacked by their fringes.' He also commented on the potential viability of the Liberal Democrats as an anti-Brexit party, saying, 'I'm not sure that they're capable of reforming as an organisation into a winning political force'. In 2024, Coghlan was elected as the Liberal Democrat MP for Dorking & Horley. He was not the only one of his party's 2024 intake to get into liberal politics because of Brexit; Liz Jarvis, now the MP for Eastleigh, wrote for *The Independent* in 2019 about her move from Labour to the Lib Dems over Europe.[3]

Coghlan split from the Renew Party in May 2018, citing differences with others in the party's leadership. Mark Kieran, who had had a long career in the civil service followed by a stint working for Camden Council, was brought in as interim chief executive of the party that same month. He says that he thought it was time for a new party because 'people were feeling hopeless'. He felt urgent action was needed, explaining that, having grown up in Northern Ireland in the 1970s and '80s, 'at a very, very fundamental level in me is an understanding of what happens when democracy and government stops working for a big chunk of the community and it turns very ugly very quickly'. There was concern about 'what Labour had done during the referendum or not done during the referendum' and overall he thought there seemed to be 'a very strong appetite for something new'. In this climate, Renew, this new party, 'seemed like a sensible thing to give a shot to,' he reckoned.

Back in the weeks after the 2017 election, Annabel Mullin, who had just contested Kensington & Chelsea for the Liberal Democrats, set up a new party. It was called Advance Together and was closer to a residents' group than a new centrist party. It was, Mullin says, 'a lot less to do with Brexit' and 'much more to do with Grenfell'. In her view, 'the response from all of the political parties was so disappointing, underwhelming. I was really horrified by their reaction.' She includes her former party in that assessment, describing the Lib Dems after the fire as having a 'tokenism about their political change and their political interaction that I found … so surface [level]'. Given this, 'we decided … we wanted to shift the shape of local politics to be more responsive and reactive to what was going on in the community'.

This new party caught Kieran's eye. 'I just liked the look of it. I thought Annabel had something to offer and I sort of suggested that she come and be part of the Renew thing,' he said. Mullin offers a similar account, recalling that Kieran 'approached me and said, "We want somebody to come and lead Renew."' She remembers him conveying that

> we want a woman. We want somebody who has had experience, who understands, you know, political parties, who obviously is somebody who supports Remain, because their piece was a lot about that, and who has an understanding of local, national politics and regional politics. And, you know, there aren't that many people who have that sort of wealth of experience.

There also weren't many who had gone through the process to 'actually set up a party, not that many people have navigated the Electoral Commission in the way I have. You know, it's a relatively rare skill set.' Mullin says she liked Kieran 'immensely, so I think he persuaded me to do it'.

And so Mullin became the interim leader of Renew in 2018. An *Evening Standard* article about Mullin's party described it as hoping 'to capture the spirit of the En Marche movement in France'.[4] However, her time in charge would be fairly short – she passed the leadership responsibility to former Conservative MEP Julie Girling in June 2019. In her time as leader, she remembers, 'we wrote our new policy position, which was in itself a huge amount of work, and then we rebranded'. They also spent a not-insignificant amount of time working out what their relationship would be to Change UK.

Mullin remembers conversations 'about joining Change UK'. She has, she says, 'a lot of experience of, like, the data behind what makes a party work' and thinks 'the boring, bureaucratic systems are absolutely fundamental to make a party work. I sat at the table and had lots of conversations with the people behind Change UK,' who, she felt

> weren't interested in that kind of side of it. They felt that actually their personality and personas were big enough for that not to be an issue. Anyone who has run in an election which isn't a safe seat, which is pretty much none of them, understand[s] the experience of what it is like to have to fight really hard for a seat when you've got nothing, no data, no people that you know.

Her review of the Change UK set was overall pretty negative: 'I think because they'd been told they could, they'd been led to believe that their personality and their Twitter following was enough to make the difference. But Twitter isn't the UK and people should stop believing it is.' Moreover, she says, 'you should never believe your own press'. She nonetheless stood at the European elections under the Change UK banner – fourth on their London list – that May. It was a 'pretty shoddy campaign,' she says.

The big electoral moment for Renew in 2019, however, came in the Newport West by-election, which took place on 4 April. The party, says Mullin, 'did a big campaign there, and that was also the first big by-election test'. She says, 'I think we got something like 7 per cent or 8 per cent of the vote.' (It was 3.7 per cent, or 879 votes.)

The seat was an easy hold for Labour and their candidate, Ruth Jones, has held it ever since. Interestingly, the Green candidate (3.9 per cent, or 924 votes) was Amelia Womack, a Newport native, who we last encountered setting up Another Europe is Possible back in Chapter 9.

Renew was funded by 'high-net-worth individuals … and some small donations across the board,' along with some membership fees. 'The entire campaign [for the] by-election in Newport was supported by one individual,' Mullin remembers. They were also hit with some fairly hefty Electoral Commission fines for a series of infractions across 2018 and 2019, and they coughed up £5,580 in July 2020.[5]

When Mullin departed Renew in the summer of 2019, she didn't leave the small party scene but instead went back to putting her energies into Advance Together. She advises me not to think too prescriptively about these party swaps (something my Labour Party rulebook-addled brain admittedly struggles with) and 'not to see it as a party. It's a method of doing political campaigning,' which she describes as useful because 'as a political entity, you have the capacity to do more, spend more and do more than you do as a non-political entity'.

At the 2019 election, Advance Together 'ran five candidates. They were not – I mean, they were people that existed. We didn't run to do anything with them. We ran to spend more money in their constituencies.' She herself racked up eighty votes in Wokingham. They ran adverts with the aim to 'stop Boris getting a large mandate'. They were, she says 'pretty visceral. And so we had some quite interesting imagery with, you know, Boris over a hospital, or Donald Trump over a hospital and the NHS being stolen by the Americans.' This Advance Together effort was funded, interestingly, in part by a donation of £20,000 from Our Future, Our Choice, given on 7 December 2019.[6]

If you didn't fancy either Renew or Advance Together, you had other options. In late 2018 it was reported in *The Times* that the businessman Simon Franks – among other things, co-founder of DVD mailing service Love Film – was set to launch a new party named United for Change. According to *The Times*, the new party would be a '"true grassroots movement" that will practise politics without tribalism, confrontation, "yelling and finger pointing"'.[7] While at the time of the reporting it had yet to get off the ground – and never would, in any meaningful sense – it did have a named chief executive, one Ryan Wain. Wain had previously worked for Labour (according to his LinkedIn, he 'took time out of my advertising career to bring some creative fizzle to a Labour Party desperately in need of it') under Miliband before coming into Franks's project.

'Rightly, you will ask some fair questions,' Wain, the Vice Admiral James Stockdale of new centrist parties, told *The Times* in 2018. 'Why should I do this? Why should I help you when I know so little about you? There isn't much about us in the public domain because we haven't spoken to a single media outfit and for good reason: we are putting substance before style.' Wain said that the party had 'created a structure to allow experts, academics and experienced practitioners to contribute. Education will be informed by teachers and educational experts, health by doctors, nurses and other health professionals, and so on.' He was at the time encouraging interest from anyone who thought they could become a 'United for Change champion'. The party never fielded candidates but garnered enough press interest to be condemned by then shadow Chancellor John McDonnell as 'a party for the few not the many' and by then shadow Health Secretary Jonathan Ashworth as 'a daft waste of time'.[8] Wain is now the executive director of the Tony Blair Institute for Global Change and sought parliamentary selection in 2024, losing out in Knowsley to the constituency's current Labour MP Anneliese Midgely.

While Renew, United for Change and Advance Together might never have been out-and-out successes, they were some of the more realised efforts in the field. In August 2017, there was not insignificant media attention devoted to the claims of James Chapman, a former adviser to the Brexit Secretary David Davies. Chapman asserted that two Cabinet ministers were interested in his proposed new party, the Democrats. He posted about it on Twitter (along with arguing that Boris Johnson should be in prison), stating that it was 'past time for sensible MPs in all parties to admit Brexit is a catastrophe, come together In new party if need be, and reverse it #euref19'.

This never came to anything, perhaps unsurprisingly. Most now credit Chapman's not-strictly-backed-up claims about his new party's support to ill-health, something which is hard – and, to a degree, taboo – to factor into analyses of politics but undeniably very necessary to a working understanding of what was going on. Everyone agrees that the Brexit years were a hectic, stressful, bizarre time, and when politics goes mad, what happens to the people whose life is politics?

Another party-via-Twitter came from the journalist Jeremy Cliffe, who was at the time Brussels bureau chief of *The Economist*. His party was called the Radicals; he described how it had come about in an October 2017 Medium post. The day prior, he said, he had been on Twitter 'depressed by the gaping void in British politics where a dynamic liberal force should be, and speculatively invited followers to email if they felt the same way'.[9] The response he received was, he said, 'overwhelming' and far beyond what he'd expected. It was clear, he wrote, that 'the absence of responsible leadership from the Conservatives, effective opposition from Labour and a distinctive, compelling offer from the Liberal Democrats [meant] people are ready for something new'.

He added that it was clear from the 'scale of this unplanned experiment that taking this forward would not be compatible with my job'. He said he found the experience 'heartening' and concluded by noting that 'the initial goal of this exercise – to show that there is an appetite for such a party – has been met, and exceeded.' And so – with, we can presume, some words having been had by his employers – died the Radicals.

The barrister Jolyon Maugham also got in on the action. His idea, he told me, 'was called Spring, the Party because, essentially, it sprang from a particular moment where Theresa May had called a general election which many in my tribe, wrongly as it transpired, felt we were going to lose and I wanted to spark some idea of hope. It was going to be a festival which might have become a political movement.' He explained that he has

> quite a number of friends who work in the music industry, and my friends in the music industry, we all felt similar unrest, and we talked about whether or not we might do something, put on something quite quickly leading up to the general election that might provide some kind of progressive rallying point. We would collect people's data, and if the thing flourished, then maybe there would be a political party at the end.

They planned to do some activities in Theresa May's constituency, but, Maugham confesses, Spring, the Party was, like Chapman and Cliffe's efforts, 'a thing that mostly existed in my head'.

The journalist Stephen Bush says that while it was understandable why some people with long-time affiliations to

Labour and the Tories were never going to choose to join the Liberal Democrats, there was a category of nascent new centrist parties that left him asking, 'Why do you think you're too good for the Lib Dems?'

'I think Jolyon Maugham's Spring is the ur-example ... you've basically got a party shot through with the idea that "Oh, the reason why the Lib Dems don't do very well is because they're crap,"' says Bush, adding that one of the underpinning assumptions of setting up such a party is a fairly hubristic 'How hard can it be, right?' As a mere glance at Change UK's logo saga will tell you, it is hard. It's not just Maugham who Bush reckons is guilty of this kind of thinking: 'Jeremy Cliffe's the Radicals is essentially, just the Lib Dems. But clearly based on this idea that the reason why the Lib Dems haven't broken through is they're no good, rather than there are hard electoral constraints here.'

The Radicals, Renew, Advance Together, Spring, the Party and United for Change all more or less lived and died within the 2017–19 parliament, but Britain finally Brexiting in January 2020 was no bar to the establishment of anti-Brexit parties. One was launched that very month: Volt UK, which is an offshoot of the pan-European federalist movement Volt Europa. They have, as of 2024, five MEPs, two from the Netherlands and three from Germany and broadly advocate closer union between EU member states. The UK branch has stood a handful of candidates at local and national elections since then, but, unsurprisingly, none have won.

Brendan Donnelly, who we met back in Chapter 1, now

leads the Rejoin EU Party. He is an old hat at this: after founding the Pro-Euro Conservative Party in 1999 (and failing to be elected at the European elections that year), he stood in the 2009 European elections as a 'Yes2Europe' candidate and was not elected. He stood again at the 2014 European elections for the 'Four Freedoms Party', a small pro-European party. He was not elected.

Rejoin EU models themselves, in terms of strategy, after an old adversary. 'We see ourselves as being parallel to UKIP,' Donnelly explains. 'Before UKIP was famous and got lots of money and got into the European Parliament, it was regarded as something of a joke.' Its analysis, however – 'that we can take votes from other supposedly anti-European parties, the Conservative Party, and we will force them, aided by the first past the post system, to move towards us,' as Donnelly explains it – was sound and proved 'very successful' at achieving their aims. 'It was precisely fear of UKIP which led Cameron to this, foolish in my view, commitment to a referendum, which he then doubly foolishly carried out.'

The Rejoin EU Party, under Donnelly and working off this UKIP logic, has contested a string of by-elections: Donnelly himself won 101 votes at the Chesham & Amersham by-election in June 2021, while Drew Galdron – fake Boris from Chapter 2 – was the party's candidate at the North Shropshire by-election that took place in December 2021. Under the name 'Bunged-up Boris', they scored fifty-eight votes. The Rejoin EU Party gained their first and only elected office in 2022, when party chairman Andy Smith became a parish councillor in Oxfordshire.

In quite a similar mould, anti-Brexit businesswoman Gina Miller has also established a party, the True and Fair Party, which was announced in late 2021. The last dregs of Renew also then merged into this party. In 2023, Miller spoke to *The Guardian* about her unhappiness with the decision of online banking company Monzo to close the True and Fair Party's account (nine other banks had previously refused to bank them). Miller said that the 'bigger issue' was 'the fact that as a new insurgent political party you have no access to banking services, which is extraordinary in a democracy'.[10] Miller was one of a handful of candidates the party stood at the 2024 general election. She picked up a respectable (but still deposit-losing) 845 votes, losing to the Liberal Democrat Helen Maguire in Epson & Ewell.

It seems fair to assume that for years to come, the Rejoin Party, the True and Fair Party, Volt UK and other small anti-Brexit parties will crop up in by-elections and contest handfuls of seats at locals and generals. Their insubstantial nature – even Miller, who became an anti-Brexit household name, couldn't keep her deposit – vindicates the focus of many in the People's Vote campaign on moving the Labour Party's position and also suggests that the way for those who are serious about moving Britain closer to Europe probably lies through the party that currently governs. And if you can't move Labour, as Chris Coghlan MP has clearly learned, you aren't too big and clever for the Liberal Democrats.

CONCLUSION

Open Britain still exists. It's run by Mark Kieran, who we last encountered during his stint as CEO of the Renew Party. He came on as COO in November 2019, when, Kieran says, Patrick Heneghan brought him in to try and put the house in order after losing the bulk of their staff very shortly before the general election. 'I went in there as his sort of right-hand man to make sure that the show was kept on the road,' is how Kieran describes it. It was reported in *The Observer* that Heneghan would stand down as acting CEO on 9 November – his tenure barely making it into the plural of 'weeks' – while, the newspaper stated, 'an investigation takes place into allegations of harassment towards female staff'.[1] Heneghan was later exonerated of any wrongdoing by the investigation. Stuart Hand, who'd been with Open Britain since it was Britain Stronger in Europe, replaced him. Rudd was reported to have quit as chair of the board on 15 November 2019.[2]

Once the election on 12 December had wrapped up, the then COO remembers that 'we then genuinely had a question to answer, which was, you know, what is the point of us? If the

People's Vote is dead as an idea, then should we just shut up shop and go home?' By the end of January, they were down to around ten staff, having had forty or fifty a few months previously.

Again, Open Britain's core asset – its data – dictated its fate. 'As you might imagine, during the People's Vote, we accumulated quite a bit of data. We had quite a few supporters. We had an email list that was, you know, about three quarters of a million people,' says Kieran. This is higher than other estimates I've heard, but it is also an estimate from later in the campaign's life cycle. You can't kill the goose with the golden egg inside it, even if you have no idea what you want the egg for.

So, the organisation kept going and changed its focus. 'My own personal view was that Brexit and what had happened since, and indeed Boris Johnson's success, was a function of a dysfunctional democracy,' says Kieran. The decision was taken 'over, I don't know, a couple of months, perhaps, that the organisation could be reoriented towards making democracy work properly'. They have, he explains to me, five strategic objectives between 2025 and 2029:

> To push back against the rise of authoritarianism around the world and particularly in this country, to encourage more ordinary people to know about their democratic rights and, importantly, how to use them. And then three things which are related to the actual electoral system, which is to change from

> first past the post to PR, to take dark money out of politics and to combat disinformation in public discourse.

Kieran is also the director of Fair Vote UK, which is the secretariat for the APPG for Fair Elections, chaired by the Labour MP Alex Sobel, who we last encountered during his time with Love Socialism Hate Brexit.

That this organisation which mostly campaigns for proportional representation is the successor organisation of the designated Remain campaign in the 2016 referendum is perhaps on the face of it odd, but British politics is full of far stranger inheritances. Unlock Democracy – 'a not-for-profit organisation which campaigns for a vibrant, inclusive democracy' and argues that we 'need a fairer voting system, a new second chamber, more devolution, and tougher rules to tackle sleaze and cronyism in politics', its website explains – is the successor organisation of the Communist Party of Great Britain, after all.[3] Perhaps it's the political equivalent of carcinisation, the tendency of many different organisms to evolve into crabs – only political organisations, given time and across a few different permutations, tend to evolve into campaigns for proportional representation.

If that's what happened to the main organisation, what about the people who made up the People's Vote campaign? The response of many of those I spoke to about the period was something akin to 'God, I've memory-holed that whole thing'. Despite its centrality in British politics just a handful of years ago, people who were intensely involved in the attempt to secure a new vote do not want to think about it. Whether people want to think about it and whether it had an impact, however, are different questions.

There are a lot of characters in this book, and most of them are still working in politics. Lara Spirit of Our Future, Our Choice is now Washington correspondent at *The Times*. Spirit's co-founder Will Dry became a SpAd to Rishi Sunak before dramatically resigning at the end of 2023; most recently, he was the subject of a Hope Not Hate report detailing his involvement with disgraced Cummings-era No. 10 adviser Andrew Sabisky.[4] Amanda Chetwynd-Cowieson is acting head of external affairs at NHS England. When interviewed for this book, Richard Brooks was director of media at the pollsters Ipsos and is now a SpAd to the Attorney General, Lord Hermer. Femi Oluwole is still @Femisorry, creating a steady stream of content. Mike Buckley of Labour for a People's Vote has a new venture called the Independent Commission on EU-UK Relations. A great many of the people who worked for the People's Vote campaign work in and around the Labour Party; the Starmer government has been good to them. Luke Myer is an MP and Tom Baldwin became the authorised biographer of the Prime Minister. Some – including Brooks, Charlie Atkins and Francis Grove-White – are SpAds and a good number work for MPs. A period in the world of the second referendum is not an uncommon thing to find stashed away at the bottom of a politico's LinkedIn.

People tend to learn lessons from earlier failed campaigns.

You can see the fingerprints of earlier experience on later actions, much in the way that you can, to my view, see echoes of Rudd and Dixon's early careers in the SDP in their post-referendum dealings. However, the journalist Stephen Bush thinks that it will be hard to see unifying factors and lessons learned from the push for a new vote because 'there were so many problems with the second referendum campaign that there are just so many different lessons that people can take from it'. As such, the people who cut their teeth there will be a 'weird tribe', Bush reckons.

I might posit that despite the home it provides to many former People's Voters, the key people who have learned lessons from the failures of this period are within the Labour Party. This partly stems from what those running the Labour Party now were doing at the time. The Labour Together group can be seen as both a fairly explicit rejection of the People's Vote and as key to the ascent of Keir Starmer. According to a 2024 profile of Morgan McSweeney, the Prime Minister's chief of staff (and former director of Labour Together)

> believes Blair has only become more removed from the reality of people's lives in the years since he has left power … the radical centrism he proposes now seems to be based on an idea that progressive parties would be better off if they simply assembled a new coalition of voters who were not so poor. Forget the council house tenants who voted Leave; target the landlords who voted Remain.[5]

If McSweeney's eventually triumphant Labour Together set saw themselves as 'trying to take back the ship,' those looking to new parties were trying to inflate a 'lifeboat' – aims, when it comes to priorities and strategy, completely at odds with one another.[6]

The rejection goes beyond Starmerism's electoral strategy – chasing 'Stevenage woman' and socially conservative potential switchers and a distinctly antagonist position towards the concerns of the liberal middle classes. While this worked to some effect at the 2024 general election, there are limits to the efficacy of this: if the People's Vote campaign succumbed to audience capture, Labour is at present going the other way and is at risk of succumbing to audience alienation.

Of course, for some, the fight is still on. They are doing what they were always doing: agitating in support of the European Union. Mike Galsworthy runs the European Movement now. Tom Brufatto is at Best for Britain, as the organisation's director of policy and research. Naomi Smith is still CEO. The rejoin gang increasingly bring to mind the Japanese soldiers in the jungle, cut off and still fighting a war long since finished. But fighting they are – while increasingly insular, prone to the problems of talking to themselves that were present even when the anti-Brexit movement was closest to the mainstream in 2018 and 2019, they are still going. They are bedded down in the culture they created; as time goes by, their bubble universe drifts ever further away from mainstream political debates and into the activist fringe, even as the possibility of moving closer to Europe is now as likely as it's been since we left.

The Lib Dems, with MPs like Chris Coghlan and Liz Jarvis on their benches, have an enduring commitment to the EU and are riding high under Ed Davey. In Labour, too, a closer relationship is being sought in policy terms, while perpetual Labour prince-across-water Andy Burnham wants to rejoin and Starmer is talking about lies on the side of a bus.

'The hardcore, the tribalists, the drum bangers, the wearers of EU flags,' says Rob Ford, 'they are not the ones who will get us over the line if we ever get another shot at this. Quite the opposite. They are a liability.' But what political scientists say doesn't particularly matter to them: to many in the most die-hard reaches of this culture, cast adrift on Steve Bray's traffic island, the particularities of Britain's relationship with the European Union became secondary some time ago, if they were ever not so. *Single Minded Rejoiners* still comes out weekly. Admirably inflation-proof, bEUrets are still for sale online, costing £10 each. Some corner of a forgotten Twitter account will be for ever following back.

NOTES

INTRODUCTION

1 https://www.ft.com/content/e02992f6-cf9e-46b3-8d45-325fb183302f
2 https://petition.parliament.uk/archived/petitions/131215
3 https://ukandeu.ac.uk/interview-pdf/?personid=46848
4 Jonathan Moss, Emily Robinson and Jake Watts, *The Politics of Feeling in Brexit Britain*, Manchester University Press, p. 78
5 https://onlinelibrary.wiley.com/doi/full/10.1111/1467-923X.13252
6 https://drb.ie/articles/identity-mines-knottier-than-yours/
7 https://ukandeu.ac.uk/brexit-witness-archive/alastair-campbell/
8 https://whatukthinks.org/eu/wp-content/uploads/2018/10/WUKT-EU-Briefing-Paper-15-Oct-18-Emotional-legacy-paper-final.pdf
9 *The Politics of Feeling*, p. 67

CHAPTER 1

1 Adam Fagan and Stijn van Kessel, *The Failure of Remain*, McGill-Queen's University Press, pp. 93–4.
2 *The Failure of Remain*, p. 94
3 *The Politics of Feeling*, p. 1
4 Ibid., p. 6, p. 69, p. 74
5 https://whatukthinks.org/eu/wp-content/uploads/2018/10/WUKT-EU-Briefing-Paper-15-Oct-18-Emotional-legacy-paper-final.pdf
6 https://eprints.lse.ac.uk/117918/1/Hobolt_losers_consent_and_emotions_brexit_published.pdf
7 Ibid.
8 *The Failure of Remain*, p. 98.
9 *The Failure of Remain*, p. 75
10 Ibid., p. 71

CHAPTER 2

1 https://www.theguardian.com/politics/2019/aug/13/brexit-remain-radicalisation-fbpe-peoples-vote
2 https://www.standard.co.uk/news/politics/eu-supergirl-activist-escorted-out-of-brexit-talks-press-conference-a3657056.html
3 https://www.theguardian.com/politics/2019/aug/13/brexit-remain-radicalisation-fbpe-peoples-vote
4 Ibid.

CHAPTER 3

1 https://eprints.lse.ac.uk/117918/1/Hobolt_losers_consent_and_emotions_brexit_published.pdf
2 https://www.theguardian.com/media/greenslade/2016/jul/04/archant-launches-pop-up-paper-to-serve-people-who-voted-remain
3 https://x.com/OhGodWhatNowPod/status/919131673924599808
4 https://www.theguardian.com/tv-and-radio/2017/oct/29/best-podcasts-of-2017-part-1-from-the-buzziest-to-politics-and-brain-food

CHAPTER 4

1 https://x.com/aaronbastani/status/1597549958991073280
2 https://www.liberation.fr/france/2012/11/05/felix-marquardt-l-art-de-l-entre-gens_858251/
3 https://www.liberation.fr/ecrans/2000/08/03/bertrand-delanoe-pro-du-porno-sans-consentement_333302/
4 https://www.vanityfair.com/news/2013/01/davos-2013-austrian-american-hip-hop-producer
5 https://www.vanityfair.fr/pouvoir/article/la-politique-le-cac-40-la-cocaine-et-puis-le-silence-felix-marquardt-raconte-son-stupefiant-destin
6 https://www.theosthinktank.co.uk/comment/2023/07/05/martin-shaw-felix-marquardt-on-religious-conversion-being-vulnerable-and-the-power-of-myths
7 https://archive.is/G4iYX#selection-2839.1-2839.267
8 https://www.washingtonpost.com/news/worldviews/wp/2015/10/29/map-these-are-the-best-and-worst-countries-for-young-people/
9 https://www.crowdfunder.co.uk/p/o-f-o-c-our-future-our-choice-stopbrexit
10 https://www.prospectmagazine.co.uk/politics/42355/seventy-per-cent-of-young-people-voted-remainlara-spirit-is-demanding-they-are-heard
11 *The Failure of Remain*, pp. 94–5

CHAPTER 5

1 https://www.amazon.com/Out-Question-Referendum-Britain-should-ebook/dp/B00IZJ14YY
2 https://www.theguardian.com/media/2010/jan/25/hugo-dixon-breakingviews-interview
3 https://infacts.org/mep-combats-brexit-myths-with-ukip-fantasies/
4 https://www.inpublishing.co.uk/articles/hugo-dixon-647
5 Ibid.
6 https://ukandeu.ac.uk/brexit-witness-archive/tom-baldwin/
7 https://www.ft.com/content/e02992f6-cf9e-46b3-8d45-325fb183302f
8 Tim Shipman, *Out*, William Collins, p. 155

CHAPTER 6

1 https://podcasts.apple.com/us/podcast/rejoin-rants-ep5-steve-bray-and-gareth-kearns/id1721654150?i=1000650883477
2 https://www.theguardian.com/world/2022/jul/26/stop-brexit-man-steve-bray-on-lies-police-powers-and-free-speech

CHAPTER 7

1 https://www.newstatesman.com/science-tech/2018/02/what-does-fbpe-mean-and-could-it-stop-brexit-history-hashtag
2 https://archive.is/9rrtc#selection-753.5-753.198

CHAPTER 8

1 https://www.bbc.com/news/uk-politics-44331013
2 https://www.theguardian.com/politics/2018/feb/08/best-for-britain-thwart-brexit-george-soros
3 https://www.ippr.org/profile/mark-malloch-brown

4 https://www.theguardian.com/politics/2017/apr/19/gina-miller-best-for-britain-tactical-voting-against-hard-brexit
5 https://www.bbc.com/news/uk-politics-44331013
6 Ibid.
7 https://ukandeu.ac.uk/brexit-witness-archive/gina-miller/
8 https://ukandeu.ac.uk/brexit-witness-archive/john-mcdonnell/
9 Anthony Barnett, *The Lure of Greatness: England's Brexit and America's Trump*, Unbound, p. 295.
10 https://www.bbc.co.uk/news/technology-50458111

CHAPTER 9

1 Andrew Murray, *Is Socialism Possible in Britain?*, Verso, p. 146
2 Andy Beckett, *The Searchers*, Penguin, p. 114
3 Owen Jones, *This Land*, Allen Lane, p. 166
4 https://ukandeu.ac.uk/brexit-witness-archive/andrew-fisher/
5 Oliver Eagleton, *The Starmer Project*, Verso, p. 76
6 https://www.qmul.ac.uk/media/news/2016/items/corbyns-labour-survey-of-post-2015-labour-members-and-supporters.html
7 https://www.theguardian.com/politics/2017/jul/17/most-labour-members-want-uk-to-remain-in-single-market
8 https://labourlist.org/2018/01/labour-members-poll-over-75-per-cent-of-want-vote-on-brexit-deal-and-to-stay-in-single-market-and-customs-union/
9 https://ukandeu.ac.uk/brexit-witness-archive/john-mcdonnell/
10 https://www.bbc.com/news/uk-england-18553933
11 *The Failure of Remain*, p. 83
12 https://labourlist.org/2019/04/love-socialism-hate-brexit-were-going-on-tour-and-want-to-meet-you/
13 https://www.jewishnews.co.uk/trade-unionist-sorry-for-pockets-full-of-soros-money-tweet/
14 https://www.theguardian.com/politics/2018/feb/24/brexit-single-market-statement-labour-campaign-jeremy-corbyn

CHAPTER 10

1 https://ukandeu.ac.uk/brexit-witness-archive/john-mcdonnell/
2 https://labourlist.org/2019/04/the-room-where-it-happened-how-we-agreed-labours-brexit-conference-policy/
3 https://labourlist.org/2018/09/labours-brexit-composite-motion-in-full/
4 Tom Baldwin, *Keir Starmer*, William Collins
5 https://labourlist.org/2019/04/the-room-where-it-happened-how-we-agreed-labours-brexit-conference-policy/
6 Baldwin, *Keir Starmer*
7 Ibid.
8 https://www.bbc.co.uk/news/uk-politics-48919695
9 *This Land*, p. 200
10 https://ukandeu.ac.uk/brexit-witness-archive/john-mcdonnell/

CHAPTER 11

1 https://www.ft.com/content/e02992f6-cf9e-46b3-8d45-325fb183302f
2 https://ukandeu.ac.uk/brexit-witness-archive/alastair-campbell/
3 https://archive.is/dnftU
4 https://www.theguardian.com/politics/2018/apr/28/brexit-not-a-done-deal-battle-to-stay-in-eu-second-referendum
5 https://archive.is/dnftU#selection-2343.340-2343.406
6 https://www.bbc.com/news/uk-42531669

7 https://www.theguardian.com/politics/2017/apr/25/pro-eu-tories-quit-open-britain-over-plans-to-oust-brexit-backing-mps
8 *Out*, p. 151
9 https://www.bbc.com/news/uk-43774200
10 https://ukandeu.ac.uk/brexit-witness-archive/alastair-campbell/

CHAPTER 12

1 Gabriel Pogrund and Patrick Maguire, *Left Out*, Bodley Head, p.
2 https://x.com/BestForBritain/status/1103602815484813313
3 https://www.bbc.co.uk/news/uk-england-cambridgeshire-45951932
4 https://www.theguardian.com/politics/2018/aug/18/founder-superdry-donates-1-million-pounds-peoples-vote-brexit-deal
5 https://www.bbc.co.uk/news/uk-politics-45235655
6 https://ukandeu.ac.uk/brexacerbation-and-the-embedding-of-brexit-in-everyday-family-life/

CHAPTER 13

1 https://www.theguardian.com/politics/2018/jun/23/brexit-protest-two-years-after-referendum
2 https://www.theguardian.com/politics/2018/oct/20/70000-demand-new-brexit-vote
3 https://www.prospectmagazine.co.uk/politics/42355/seventy-per-cent-of-young-people-voted-remainlara-spirit-is-demanding-they-are-heard
4 https://www.theguardian.com/politics/2019/mar/20/peoples-vote-march-200-coaches-heading-to-london-organisers-say
5 https://www.bbc.com/news/uk-45925542
6 https://www.standard.co.uk/news/uk/delia-smith-to-lead-march-for-a-people-s-vote-on-brexit-deal-a3962206.html
7 https://x.com/DMinghella/status/1053754449853276217lang=en
8 https://www.belfasttelegraph.co.uk/opinion/news-analysis/lindy-mcdowell-i-am-a-remainer-but-its-so-wrong-to-sneer-at-brexiteers-as-racist-old-thick-male-and-irrelevant/37463008.html
9 https://www.telegraph.co.uk/travel/ski/news/best-ski-resorts-book-train-uk-europe/
10 https://www.crowdfunder.co.uk/p/wooferendum
11 https://www.thetimes.com/travel/its-not-just-the-middletons-i-took-my-own-dog-skiing-heres-how-jglvdnpmw
12 https://www.theguardian.com/lifeandstyle/gallery/2018/oct/07/bark-if-you-want-to-stop-brexit-wooferendum-in-pictures

CHAPTER 14

1 https://ukandeu.ac.uk/brexit-witness-archive/caroline-lucas/
2 *Out*, p. 155
3 https://inews.co.uk/news/politics/peterborough-by-election-candidate-femi-oluwole-remain-anti-brexit-vote-289852?srsltid=AfmBOopHJx8-3r2q32r6ewGQUpBLcHV5hWotMP7BemIyotrBIGhkLgrc
4 https://www.independent.co.uk/voices/peterborough-by-election-femi-oluwole-change-uk-lib-dems-labour-farage-brexit-a8908801.html
5 https://inews.co.uk/news/politics/peterborough-by-election-candidate-femi-oluwole-remain-anti-brexit-vote-289852?srsltid=AfmBOopHJx8-3r2q32r6ewGQUpBLcHV5hWotMP7BemIyotrBIGhkLgrc

CHAPTER 15

1 https://www.theguardian.com/politics/2020/aug/27/labour-official-denies-grand-plan-sabotage-corbyn-2017-election-bid-patrick-heneghan
2 https://www.bbc.com/news/uk-england-london-49058433

3 https://www.aljazeera.com/news/2019/7/20/boris-blimp-at-london-rally-as-thousands-march-against-brexit
4 https://ukandeu.ac.uk/brexit-witness-archive/alastair-campbell/
5 *Out*, p. 160
6 https://archive.is/dnftU
7 https://www.theguardian.com/politics/2019/oct/28/peoples-vote-senior-figures-forced-out
8 https://ukandeu.ac.uk/brexit-witness-archive/alastair-campbell/
9 https://order-order.com/2019/10/29/peoples-vote-heavies-refuse-baldwin-mcgrory-entry-rudd-meeting/
10 *Out*, p. 155
11 https://archive.is/dnftU

CHAPTER 16

1 https://www.theguardian.com/politics/2019/aug/11/caroline-lucas-calls-for-emergency-female-cabinet-to-block-no-deal-brexit
2 https://www.wired.com/story/change-uk-independent-group-logo-eu-elections/
3 https://ukandeu.ac.uk/brexit-witness-archive/andrew-fisher/
4 Patrick Maguire and Gabriel Pogrund, *Get In*, Bodley Head, p. 41
5 https://www.theguardian.com/commentisfree/2018/aug/24/labour-party-split-sdp-tories-england
6 https://ukandeu.ac.uk/brexit-witness-archive/andrew-fisher/

CHAPTER 17

1 https://www.standard.co.uk/news/politics/european-elections-2019-ukeup-party-vying-for-votes-by-being-the-most-remain-a4148381.html
2 https://www.ft.com/content/ec334a98-af55-11e7-aab9-abaa44b1e130
3 https://www.independent.co.uk/voices/brexit-labour-lib-dems-final-say-referendum-vince-cable-jeremy-corbyn-a8707616.html
4 https://www.standard.co.uk/hp/front/former-lib-dem-launches-new-political-party-to-challenge-outdated-system-a3677471.html
5 https://www.electoralcommission.org.uk/political-registration-and-regulation/our-enforcement-work/investigations
6 https://morningstaronline.co.uk/article/f/ofoc-there-goes-centrists
7 https://archive.is/iO3AV#selection-1539.20-1539.139
8 https://www.theguardian.com/politics/2018/apr/08/a-daft-waste-of-time-labour-pours-scorn-on-new-centrist-party
9 https://medium.com/@JeremyCliffe/next-steps-for-the-radicals-on-accidentally-starting-a-political-party-ea306843bbae
10 https://www.theguardian.com/business/2023/jul/28/gina-miller-true-and-fair-party-monzo-bank-account

CONCLUSION

1 https://www.theguardian.com/uk-news/2019/nov/09/peoples-vote-chief-takes-leave-of-absence-after-harassment-claims
2 https://www.theguardian.com/politics/2019/nov/15/roland-rudd-exits-peoples-vote-amid-continuing-rancour
3 https://unlockdemocracy.org.uk/about-us
4 https://investigations.hopenothate.org.uk/andrew-sabisky-westminster-network/
5 https://unherd.com/2024/05/the-mcsweeney-project/
6 *Get In*, p. 41

ACKNOWLEDGEMENTS

I wanted to call this book *Stars in Their Eyes*, but my publisher told me that would make people think of singing contests, so the first thanks goes to my friend Charles White, who came up with the title. Thanks are also owed to Rida Vaquas – without her generous and useful advice about the vicissitudes of book publishing, you probably wouldn't be reading this now.

I'd like to thank Megan Corton Scott, Alistair Strathern and Drs Jack Kerwin and Max Shock for their friendship, kindness and patience – all of which were demonstrated when they let me stay with them while I was conducting interviews for this book in London but had inconveniently decided to live in Kent.

More generally, I'd be nowhere without my friends, and so, in no particular order, thanks are due to Caitlin Prowle, Kieran Maxwell, Peter Whitehead, Heather Lafferty, Sam Osborne, Nick Garland, Francis Getliffe, Beth Cheshire, Hannah Read, Leigh Deabill, Lottie Sellers, Gareth Bentley, Eve Willis, Nicole Kempis, Sophie Donnelly, Clara Collingwood, George Morris, Sigrid Koerner and many others I'm probably rudely forgetting for their support, wise and less-wise counsel, and amenable rent splits over many years. Professionally, I'd be nowhere without the good auspices of Suzanne Bold, Hana Al-Izzi and Elliot Chappell, whose kind turns I may repay someday, but frankly, it's unlikely at this stage. Thanks also to everyone who read the manuscript (or, in earlier stages, simply riffed) and were so generous with their time and advice.

Thanks are also due to my parents, who, after a lifetime of sound parenting, also let me stay in their house and not talk to anyone or be tempted to go to the pub while I wrote this. Thanks, of course, to my fiancé – and, more importantly, *Renewal* co-editor – David Klemperer, who took having his domestic life soundtracked by recordings of interviews with Tom Baldwin fairly well.

Finally, I am sincerely grateful to everyone who spoke to me for this book.

INDEX